REVIEWS:

"*More Guitar Chords and Accompaniment* is perhaps the answer to anyone who composes on guitar, or who wants to expand their basic chord roots.....easily. It is intelligently organized and will actually help anyone looking to improve their guitar playing. There are some nice guitar chord books on the market, but this one is without a doubt one of the best, perhaps THE best! We highly recommend this to anyone who wants to expand their guitar-playing ability."

—Bob Everhart
Tradition Magazine, Sept.-Oct. 1999

"A clearly written book which takes the beginner to the next level in developing a solid chord vocabulary."

—Don Latarski
Author of "The Ultimate Guitar Chord Big Book"

"A wonderful follow-up book to *Guitar Chords and Accompaniment*. A book for all levels of players—very well thought out."

—Ron Middlebrook
Author/Publisher, Centerstream Publishing

"While the first book effectively sought to get the beginning guitarist up and running, and gave the basic skills needed to accompany, *More Guitar Chords and Accompaniment* builds on those skills to make the musician more versatile and confident playing different styles of music."

—Tom Person
Laughing Bear Newsletter

More Guitar Chords and Accompaniment

2nd Edition

by

Yoichi Arakawa

SIX STRINGS
MUSIC PUBLISHING

Published by
Six Strings Music Publishing
P.O. Box 7718, Torrance, CA 90504-9118, U.S.A.
contact@sixstringsmusicpub.com
http://www.sixstringsmusicpub.com

First Printing 1999
Second Printing 2002, completely revised and expanded

Printed in the United States of America

Cover Illustrations by Frank Foster

ISBN: 1-891370-11-1

Publisher's Cataloging-in-Publication
(Provided by Quality Books, Inc.)

Arakawa, Yoichi.
    More guitar chords and accompaniment : step up your
chord vocabulary and accompaniment skills / by Yoichi
Arakawa. -- 2nd ed.
    p. cm. -- (Guitar chords and accompaniment)
    ISBN: 1-891370-11-1

    1. Guitar--Methods--Self-instruction. 2. Guitar--
Chord diagrams. I. Title.

MT588.A73 2001   787.87'9368
                              QBI01-700409

TABLE OF CONTENTS

INTRODUCTION

Welcome to *More Guitar Chords and Accompaniment*! As a continuation of my introductory book, *Guitar Chords and Accompaniment* (ISBN: 1-891370-10-3), this book goes into more detail about the areas covered earlier and also introduces some new materials to help expand your chord vocabulary and improve your accompaniment skills. Although this book is a sequel and studying *Guitar Chords and Accompaniment* first is highly recommended, it is suitable for anyone who knows basic open chords, has a basic understanding of music theory, and is able to read music.

Chapter 1 presents some music terms and concepts that were not previously covered: *changes of tempo, dynamics, articulation, time signature, simple and compound meters* and *chord symbols*. This chapter has been newly added in this revised edition not only to introduce you to some new music elements and theory, but also to help you interpret and play music with more insight.

Chapter 2 first briefly reviews how to read a chord diagram and slash notation, and introduces you to several *muting techniques*—methods to prevent unwanted strings from ringing. Then the chapter presents new chords and strumming patterns in various time signatures.

Chapter 3 continues to introduce you to more new and advanced chords, along with new fingerstyle patterns in a variety of meters such as 2/4, 3/4, 4/4, 3/8, 6/8, 12/8, and 2/2.

In Chapter 4, you will learn how to transpose various open and barre chords to different keys along the fingerboard. You will first study several principles and techniques for moving a chord, then numerous examples and exercises will follow.

Chapter 5 will immensely expand your chord vocabulary by presenting various alternative ways to play many of the open and slash chords introduced in these two books.

Chapter 6 presents accompaniment examples for various styles of music including *blues, rock, folk, country, classical, jazz,* and *Latin*. The examples apply chords and accompaniment patterns presented thus far, but also have been carefully created and arranged to demonstrate how you can create your own accompaniment for different musical styles.

Along the way, you may feel overwhelmed with practicing and just thinking about conquering all the chords in all positions and all keys. Don't worry. You won't need to memorize or remember all the possible alternative forms of the C6 chord, for example, all at once. Select and practice only those chord shapes that appeal to your ears. Or, you can refer back to them whenever you are writing a song and need something different. Gradually build and create your own favorite versions suited to your needs over a period of time and as you pursue a particular musical direction.

Good luck! I sincerely hope you will have a lot of fun and further advance your guitar-playing skills by working with this book!

EQUIPMENT YOU'LL NEED

GUITAR	METRONOME	PICK

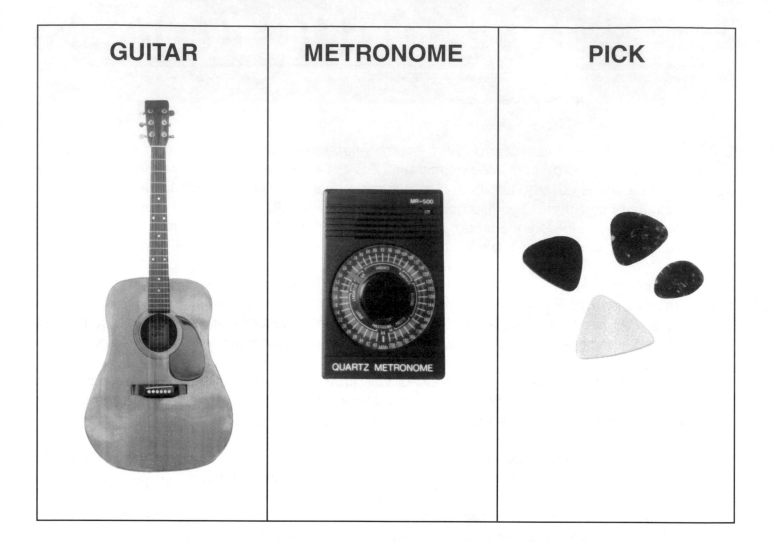

OPTIONAL EQUIPMENT

MUSIC STAND	FOOTSTOOL	CAPO

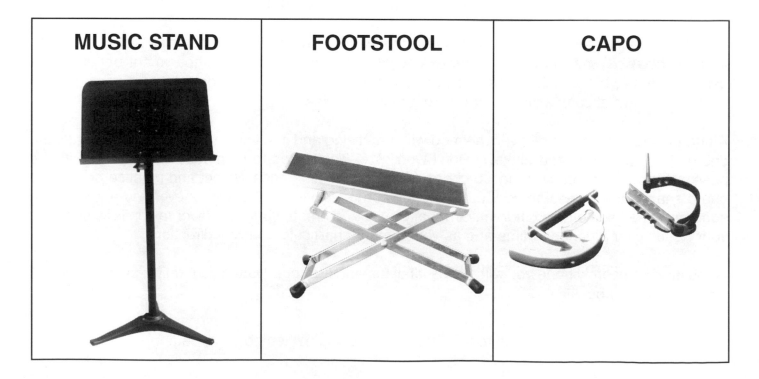

CHAPTER 1

MORE BASICS AND THEORY

In this chapter you will learn some music terms and theory that were not covered in the introductory book, *Guitar Chords and Accompaniment*. Commonly found in a songbook or lead sheet, the terms and symbols explained in this chapter are directions that help a performer to play music better and more expressively. The three types of directions relate to *changes of tempo, dynamics,* and *articulation.* As subtle as these directions may look, they are important elements that breathe life into music. As a matter of fact, without them, music would become toneless and lifeless. In addition, you will review and learn more about *time signature, meter,* and *chord symbols.*

CHANGES OF TEMPO

As you may remember, *tempo* refers to the speed at which music is to be played. The tempo is indicated at the beginning of the music by a descriptive term and/or a metronomic setting. Although the initial tempo is normally maintained throughout the performance, it can sometimes be slowed down or accelerated intentionally to create a certain mood or effect. For instance, a portion of a song may speed up gradually to heighten the excitement, or the tempo may slow down at the end of a section to create a dramatic feeling. The following Italian terms or their symbols are commonly used to change the tempo during the performance:

TERMS	MEANING	SYMBOLS
Rallentando	Slow down	*rall.*
Ritardando	Slow down gradually	*rit.*
Allargando	Slow down with increasing loudness	*allarg.*
Accelerando	Accelerate	*accel.*
Stringendo	Play at a faster tempo	*string.*
Fermata	Hold	⌒
Rubato	Play freely (free tempo)	*rubato*
A tempo	In tempo (return to the original tempo)	*a tempo*

DYNAMICS

Dynamics refers to the degree of loudness or softness with which the music is to be played. You rarely hear music at the same level of loudness throughout a performance. One section may be played softly, followed by a bridge part played with more intensity. Dynamics often help to make music and a performance more expressive and dramatic. Below are some of the dynamics marks commonly used:

TERMS	MEANING	SYMBOLS
pianissimo	Very soft	*pp*
piano	Soft	*p*
mezzo piano	Moderately soft	*mp*
mezzo forte	Moderately loud	*mf*
forte	Loud	*f*
fortissimo	Very loud	*ff*

Just as tempo can be changed during a performance, dynamics can also be changed. Changes in dynamics are indicated by the following terms and symbols:

TERMS	MEANING	SYMBOLS
crescendo	Gradually louder	*cresc.,* <
decrescendo	Gradually softer	*decresc.,* >
diminuendo	Gradually diminishing softer	*dim.*

ARTICULATION

Articulation refers to the way a note or chord is to be played or attacked. In Section 2-5 of the introductory book, you learned one such articulation, *accent* (>), which means to put a stronger emphasis on a note or a chord. There are many other articulations, and on the next page, commonly used articulations and their symbols are summarized.

TERMS	MEANING	SYMBOLS
accent (sforzando) [1]	The note is to be attacked strongly	> or _sf_
forzando (forzato) [2]	The note is to be attacked more strongly	^ _fz_
sforzato	The note is to be attacked most strongly	^ _sfz_
staccato	The note is to be played short	
legato (tenuto) [3]	The note is to be played long and held for its full value	
slur	A group of notes is to be played in a smooth, continuous way	

Notes: 1. *The symbol > is called either an accent or sforzando mark.*
2. *The symbol ^ is called either a wedge or forzando mark.*
3. *Legato is also sometimes called tenuto.*

Sometimes the articulation marks above are used in combination, as in the following:

SYMBOLS	MEANING
	The note is to be attacked strongly and played short
	The note is to be attacked more strongly and played short
	The note is to be attacked strongly and held long
	The note is to be attacked most strongly and held long

TIME SIGNATURE AND METER

Time signature, if you recall from the introductory book, is a fraction placed at the beginning of music that indicates how many counts are in each measure and what kind of note will represent a count. For instance, in 4/4, there are four counts in a measure and a quarter note receives one count. Likewise, in 3/4, there are three counts in a measure and a quarter note gets one count. The previous book presented only these two most popularly used time signatures. There are, however, many other time signatures and you will study some of them in this book. In order to understand them better, let's first look at the underlying concept of time signature, *meter*.

Meter

Music is played with a definite rhythm or beat. It is the basic pulse to which you naturally tap your foot or dance when you hear music. When you turn on your metronome, you hear a succession of beats that is regular and steady like the ticking of a watch, no matter how fast or slow it is set. Rather than having a long and continuous chain of beats, they can be organized—and therefore better understood—by using measures and bar lines. If you recall, for example, in 4/4, there are *four* regular beats arranged in a measure, which is separated by bar lines from the adjacent measures. Similarly, in 3/4, each measure is arranged to include *three* beats. This arrangement of beats into measures, or the organizational pattern of pulses, is called *meter*. And the time signature indicates how the beats are arranged, or what meter the music is based on.

Any number of basic beats can be put in a measure. In *duple* meters, for instance, there are two basic beats in a measure. *Triple* meters have three basic beats per measure, *quadruple* meters have four basic beats per measure, *quintuple* meters have five basic beats per measure, and so forth. So, 3/4 time, which has three beats per measure is said to be a triple meter. What would you call 4/4, which has four beats per measure? Yes, it is called a quadruple meter. Moreover, the basic beats in a measure can be further subdivided into two or three parts.

Simple Meter or Simple Time

In *simple meter* or *simple time*, each basic beat in a measure is *divisible* into *two* of the next smaller note values. In 4/4, for instance, the basic beat is a quarter note, which can be divided into two eighth notes—the next smaller note value of a quarter note. Below are four examples of simple meters with different time signatures. Notice how each basic beat is divisible into two of the next smaller note values.

Compound Meter or Compound Time

In *compound meter* or *compound time*, each beat is subdivided into *three* parts instead of two. For instance, 6/8—which is one of the common compound time signatures—first tells us that there are six counts per measure, with an eighth note receiving one count. Unless the tempo is extremely slow, however, 6/8 is typically beaten or conducted in *two* main beats: **ONE**-&-ah, **TWO**-&-ah, **ONE**-&-ah, **TWO**-&-ah, etc.—that is, *three eighth notes to a beat*. The way you hear and subdivide each beat is the same as *the eighth-note triplet* you learned in Section 3-7 of *Guitar Chords and Accompaniment*.

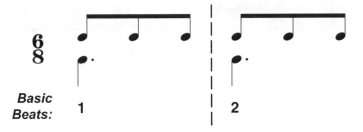

As you can see above, in 6/8 there are two basic beats and each beat is equivalent to three eighth notes or one dotted quarter note. Similarly, as shown below, in 9/8 nine eighth notes are arranged in three parts. And in 12/8, there are four basic beats, with each divisible into three eighth notes.

Some of the common simple and compound meters are summarized in the chart below:

METERS	SIMPLE			COMPOUND		
Duple:	$\frac{2}{2}$	$\frac{2}{4}$	$\frac{2}{8}$	$\frac{6}{2}$	$\frac{6}{4}$	$\frac{6}{8}$
Triple:	$\frac{3}{2}$	$\frac{3}{4}$	$\frac{3}{8}$	$\frac{9}{2}$	$\frac{9}{4}$	$\frac{9}{8}$
Quadruple:	$\frac{4}{2}$	$\frac{4}{4}$	$\frac{4}{8}$	$\frac{12}{2}$	$\frac{12}{4}$	$\frac{12}{8}$

CHORD SYMBOLS

The way a chord is indicated or written sometimes varies from one musician to another, and from one book to another. Although the chord symbols appearing in this and the previous book are common and frequently used, you may find different notations in other instruction books, lead sheets or songbooks. The chart below lists some of the other chord symbols you may encounter from time to time and have trouble recognizing. For simplicity, all chords are written in the key of C.

COMMON SYMBOLS	OTHER CHORD SYMBOLS
C	C triad, CMa, CMA, CMaj
Cmaj7	CM, CM7, C△, C△7, C7̶
C(add9)	Cadd9, C(addD), C2
C $^6_9$	C6/9, C6(add9), C6(9)
Csus4	Csus
C5	C(no 3rd), C(omit 3), C(−3), C(no E)
Cm	Cmin, Cmi, C−
Cm7	Cmin7, Cmi7, C−7
Cm(maj7)	Cmi(MA7), C−(ma7), C−(△7), C−7̶, C−(♯7)
Cm9	Cmin9, Cmi9, C−9, Cm7(9)
Cm7♭5	Cmi7♭5, Cm7(♭5), C∅7, C∅, C−7♭5
C7	CDOM7
C9	CDOM9, C7(9), C7(add9)
C7sus4	C7sus, C7(sus4), C4
C+	Caug, CAUG
C°7	Cdim7, CDIM7
C7♭9	C7(♭9), C7−9, C7(−9)
C7♯9	C7(♯9), C7+9, C7(+9)

CHAPTER 2
MORE CHORDS AND STRUMMING

The next two chapters introduce some new chords that were not included in *Guitar Chords and Accompaniment*. Additionally, you will learn new strumming and fingerstyle patterns in various rhythms and time signatures. Before we jump into the new chords and accompaniment patterns, let's briefly review the *chord diagram* and *slash notation* used throughout this book. Then, we'll discuss *muting techniques*—methods to prevent unwanted strings from ringing.

CHORD DIAGRAM

A *chord diagram,* or a *chord frame,* shows a portion of the guitar fingerboard. The six vertical lines represent the strings, from left to right, 6th, 5th, 4th, 3rd, 2nd, and 1st. The horizontal lines represent frets. The thick horizontal line at the top is the nut. The black dots placed on the vertical lines represent the locations at which the left-hand fingers should be placed.

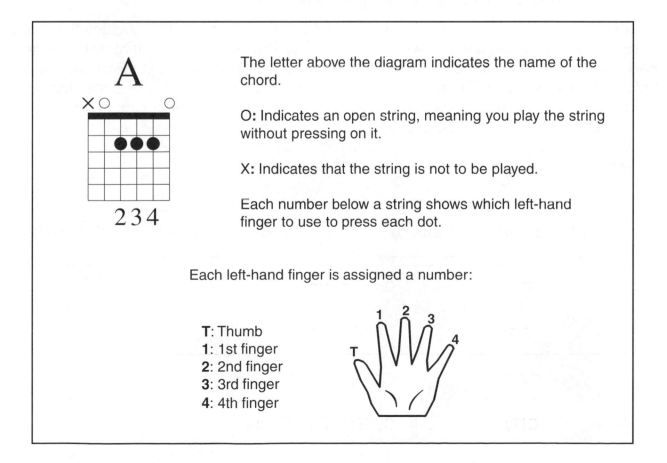

The letter above the diagram indicates the name of the chord.

O: Indicates an open string, meaning you play the string without pressing on it.

X: Indicates that the string is not to be played.

Each number below a string shows which left-hand finger to use to press each dot.

Each left-hand finger is assigned a number:

T: Thumb
1: 1st finger
2: 2nd finger
3: 3rd finger
4: 4th finger

16

SLASH NOTATION

Instead of oval-shaped notes, *slashes* will be used in a rhythm chart to indicate strumming. Just like a note, a slash indicates how long or for how many counts you sustain the chord. The following chart shows the different kinds of slashes and their corresponding notes and counts.

Regular Notation	o	♩	♩	♪	♫	♩.	♩.	♪.
Slash Notation								
Counts	4	2	1	1/2	1/4	3	1 1/2	3/4

MUTING TECHNIQUES

As shown on the previous page, an X mark on a chord diagram indicates that the string is not to be played. When the notes are not compatible with a chord, it is important to prevent them from sounding. If the 6th or both the 6th and 5th strings are not to be played, you can simply *avoid hitting* them. Sometimes, however—especially when you're strumming enthusiastically—you may hit these strings by accident. In such a case, you can deaden or mute the sound by *lightly touching* the unwanted strings using one of the following techniques.

1. Mute with Your Left-Hand Thumb

As an example, finger the Am chord on your guitar. Up until now, you've avoided the X-marked 6th string simply by not playing it. As an alternative, you can extend your left-hand thumb from the neck, roll it a little toward the 6th string, and *lightly touch* the string (as shown in the Am picture below) so that it will sound muted even if you strum it. Be careful *not to press* the string or it will produce a sound instead of being deadened. Depending on the size of your hand, the width of your guitar neck, and what kind of chord you are holding, you may not always find this technique practical, but this method is very useful and utilized by many players. And as you can see in the D7 picture, you can even mute more than one string simultaneously!

Am
(thumb muting 6th string)

D7
(thumb muting 6th and 5th strings)

2. Mute by Tilting or Extending a Fretting Finger

You can mute any string adjacent to one you are fretting by either tilting or slightly extending your finger toward the unwanted string and *lightly* touching it. As you can seen in the Gsus4 picture below, the 5th string can be muted by tilting your 3rd finger toward the floor and lightly touching the string. Similarly, in the C chord picture, notice how the tip of the 3rd finger is slightly extended toward the 6th string to lightly touch and mute it. This requires a little practice until your 3rd finger can find a perfect position to mute the string properly each time. Once you master each technique, however, you can easily apply it to many other chords.

Gsus4
(3rd finger muting 5th string)

C
(3rd finger muting 6th string)

3. Mute with Other Available Fingers

When the chord you are holding does not use all of your left-hand fingers, you can sometimes use them to mute any unwanted string(s). Look at the example below and see how the 4th finger is extended to mute the 6th string of Am. Admittedly, the technique is more often used in playing other types of chords than open chords, such as the one-note or two-note chords that you would play in funk, rock, and jazz fusion musical styles. Nevertheless, it may be worthwhile to experiment with this technique and see how you can use it in your own playing.

Am
(4th finger muting 6th string)

2-1 MAJOR(add9)

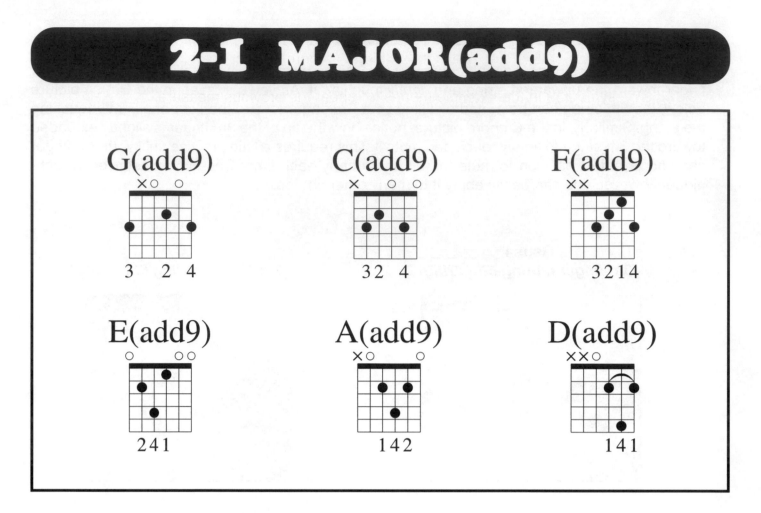

Section 2-1 presents six *major(add9)* chords above and three strumming patterns in sixteenth-note slashes below. Add9 chords can add a nice and beautiful sound and are often used in contemporary rock or pop music. As in the introductory book, whenever you learn a new chord or accompaniment pattern, be sure to play it *very slowly* at first, ensuring correct learning.

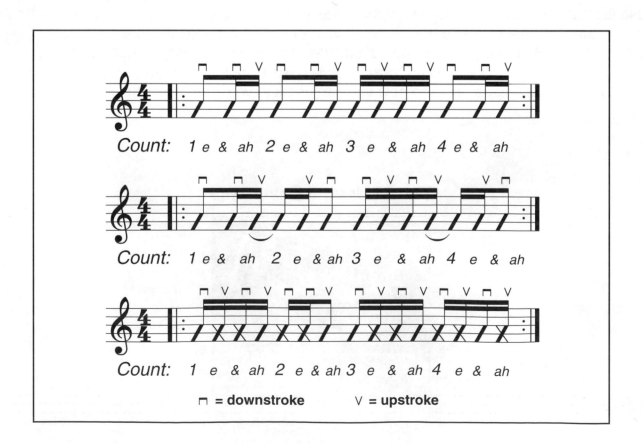

If you are comfortable with playing each chord and accompaniment pattern, try the following four exercises. Either pick a pattern and play it through each progression or combine several strumming patterns of your choice as shown in the example. Remember to *always* use a metronome, count, and play slowly. The symbol, ✗ in the example means to repeat the previous measure.

Example:

1

2

3

4
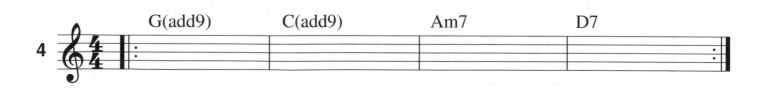

2-2 MINOR(add9)

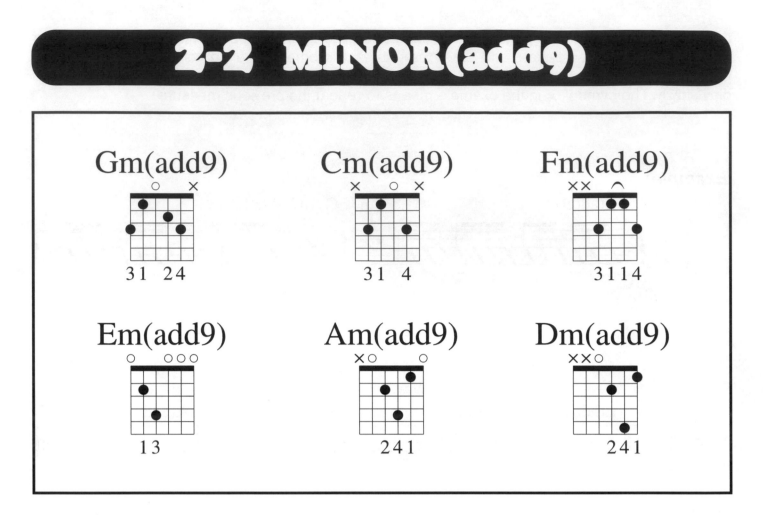

Here are six *minor(add9)* chords and three strumming patterns with dotted-eighth-note slashes. A dotted eighth note, if you remember, receives 3/4 count and is sustained for **e-&-ah** in each pattern below. Count accurately and practice each pattern very slowly at first.

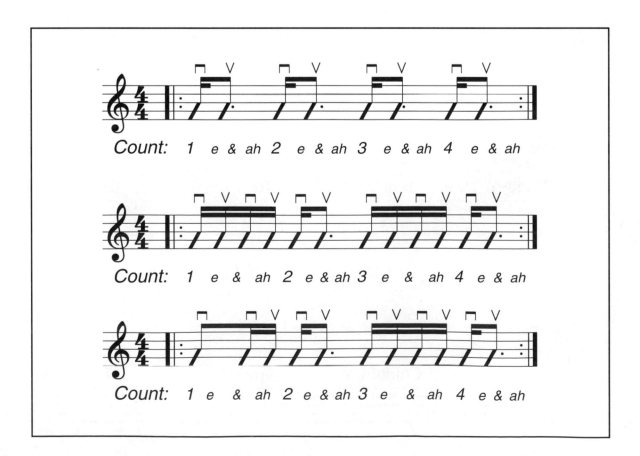

After you become comfortable with playing the chords and accompaniment patterns, move on to the following exercises. As shown in the example, you can combine several patterns or play one pattern throughout each exercise.

Example:

1

2

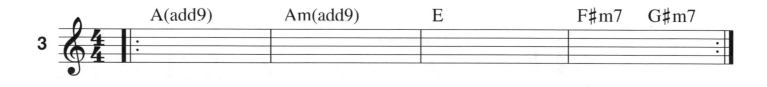

3

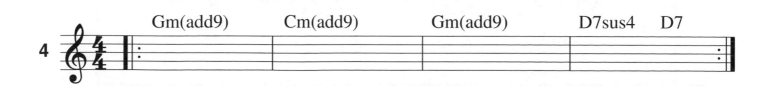

4

2-3 MAJOR SIX-NINE

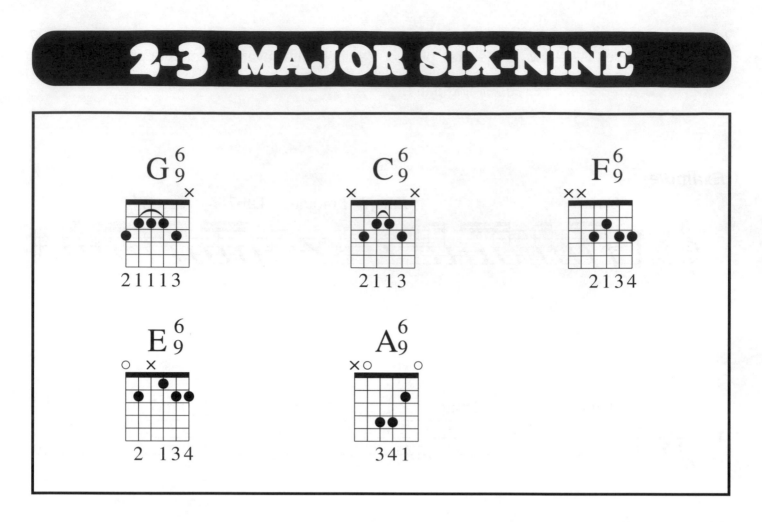

In this section, five *major six-nine* chords and three strumming patterns are presented. Notice there are dotted-eighth-note slashes again in each pattern. Study carefully where to attack and how long to sustain the chord. For instance, in the first pattern, the dotted-eighth-note slash is to be attacked on each beat and sustained for **1-e-&**.

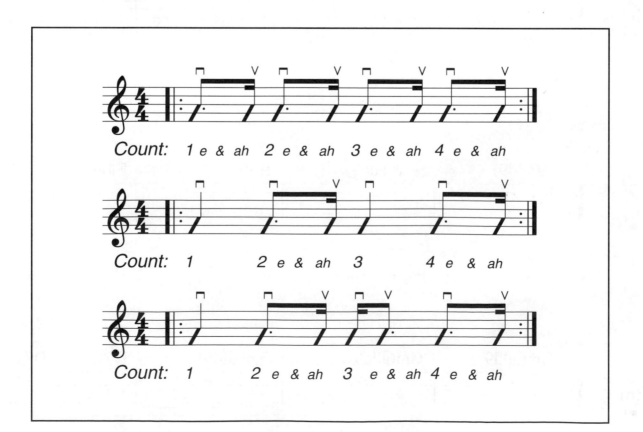

A pattern based on a dotted eighth note followed by a sixteenth note (♪ ♪) creates a certain *swing* feel and is often played in such musical styles as shuffle, blues, and jazz. When you are comfortable with the chords and patterns, practice the following exercises. Use a metronome and experiment with various combinations of strumming patterns.

Example:

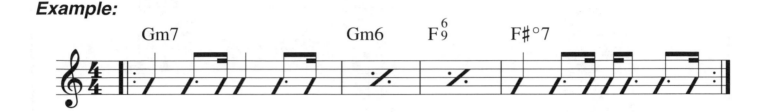

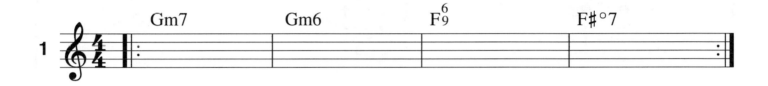

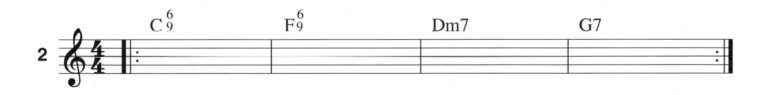

2-4 MINOR SIX-NINE

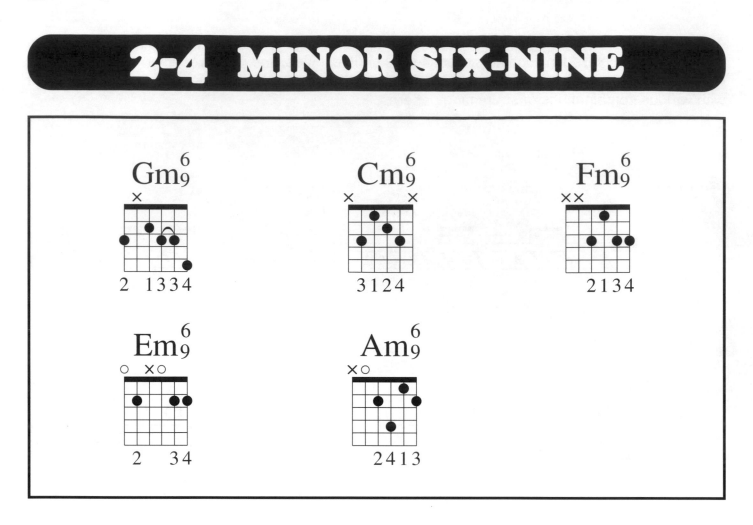

Five *minor six-nine* chords and three strumming patterns are introduced in this section. As shown in the last pattern below, combining various sixteenth-note and eighth-note slashes can create many new and different accompaniment patterns. Try making up some of your own original patterns in this way.

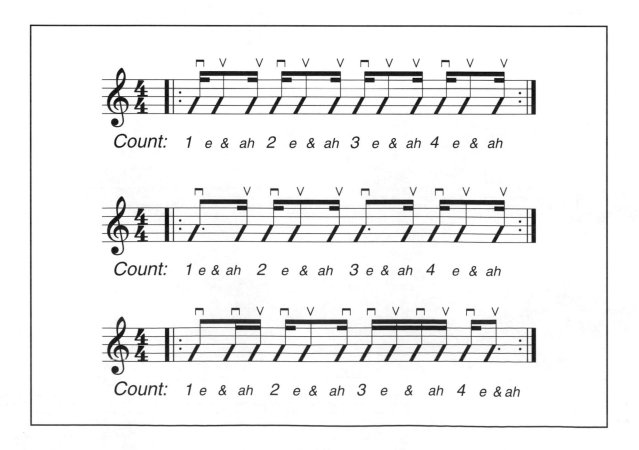

When you become comfortable with playing the minor six-nine chords and each strumming pattern, move on to the following exercises. Make sure you use a metronome, count accurately, and practice repeatedly until you can play each progression flawlessly.

Example:

1

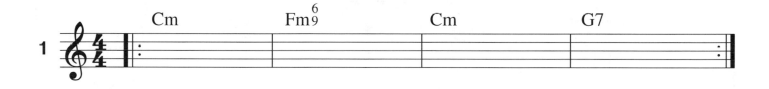

2

3

4

2-5 MAJOR 9

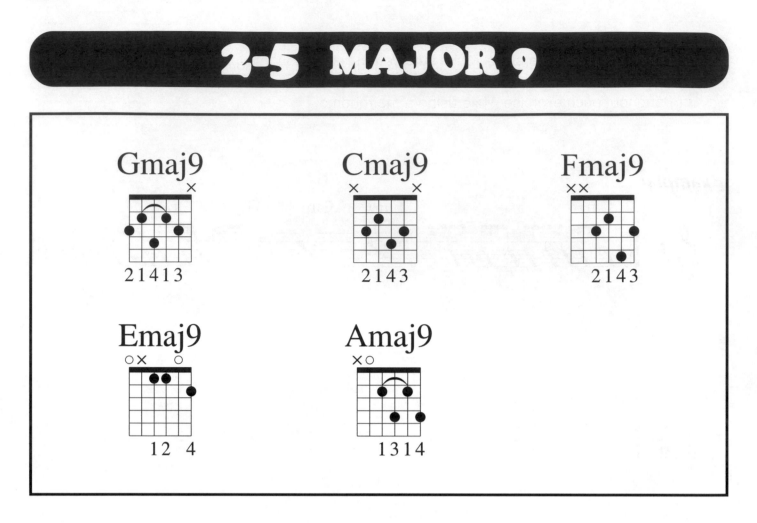

This section presents *major 9* chords. Notice the *eighth rests* in each strumming pattern below. Be sure to mute the sound completely at these rests either by releasing the pressure of your left hand or by placing your right hand lightly on the strings.

The major 9 chords are commonly played in jazz and Latin music. Watch out for those strings that are not to be played. After you become comfortable with playing the chords and accompaniment patterns, try the following exercises. Combine various patterns of your choice or pick one pattern and play it throughout each exercise while using a metronome.

Example:

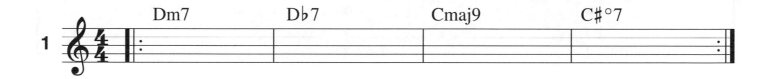

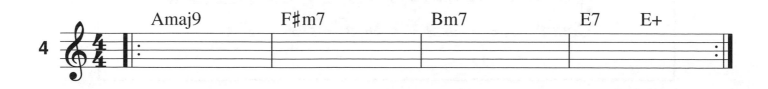

28

2-6 MINOR 9

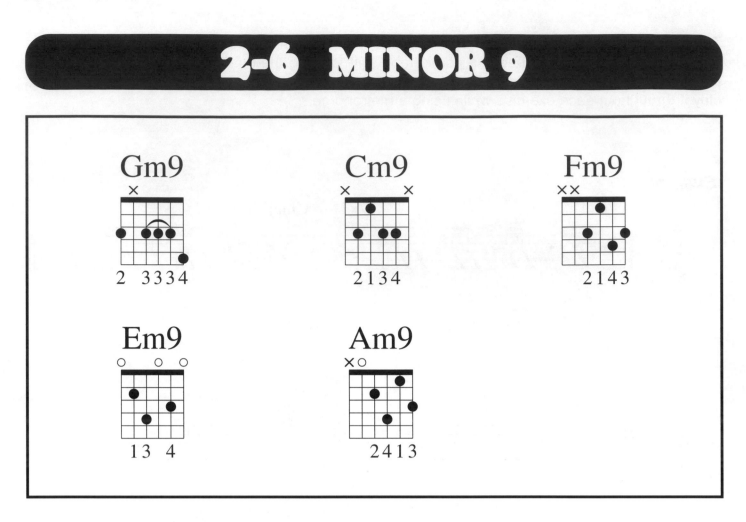

This section introduces *minor 9* chords and strumming patterns with *sixteenth rests*. A sixteenth rest, if you recall, tells you not to play for **1/4 count**. Because this rest is very short, it is probably more practical to mute the sound by releasing the pressure of your fretting hand off a barre chord than by playing an open chord and placing your right hand on the strings.

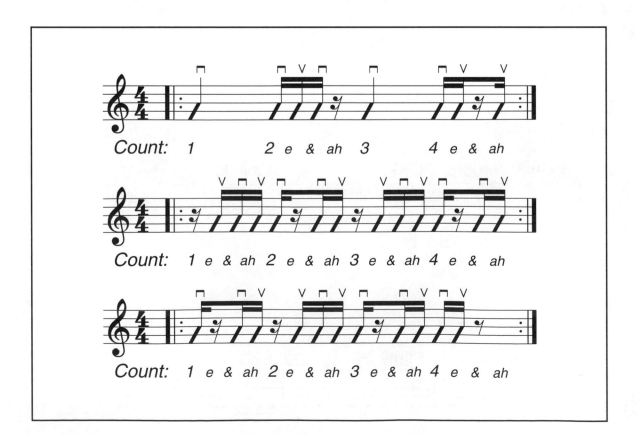

Play each pattern on the previous page even slower than usual. To make each rest clear and distinct, the slash preceding it should be played short. When you are comfortable with playing these chords and patterns, move on to the exercises below. Use a metronome and try each progression with various combinations of strumming patterns.

Example:

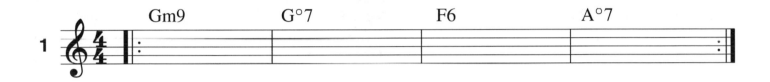

2-7 DOMINANT 9

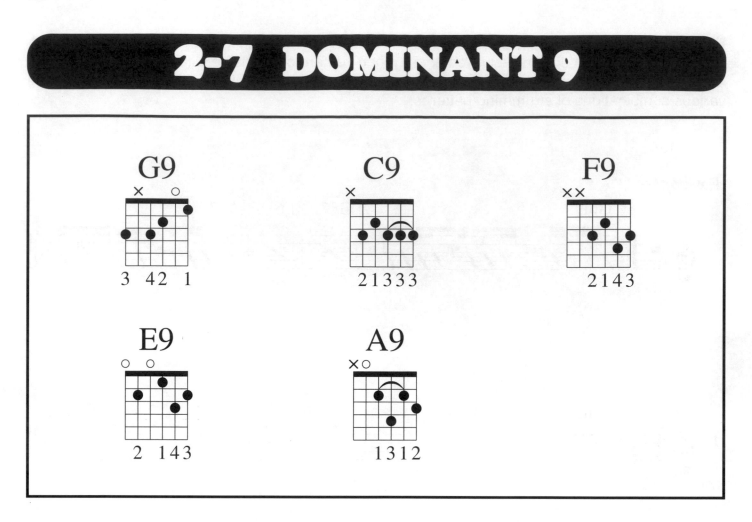

Above are five *dominant 9* chords that are popularly played in rock, funk, jazz, and Latin music. The new strumming patterns below include sixteenth rests at different places than those you saw in Section 2-6.

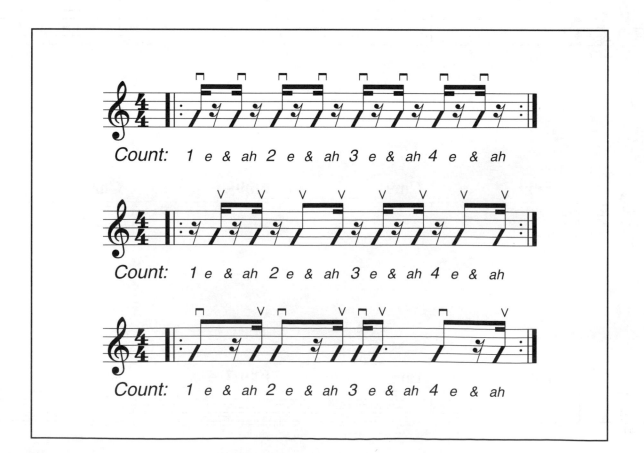

Don't let these rests catch you off guard! Just *slow everything down* and take one beat at a time, making sure you play and rest properly. If you are comfortable with playing each chord and strumming pattern, move on to the following exercises. Play each progression through with one strumming pattern, as shown in the example, or combine several patterns.

Example:

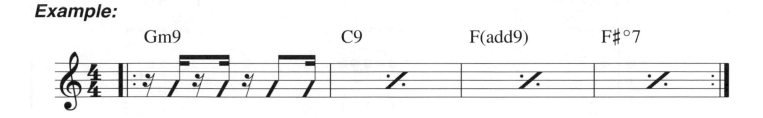

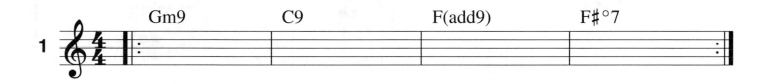

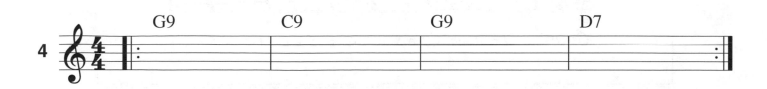

2-8 DOMINANT 9sus4

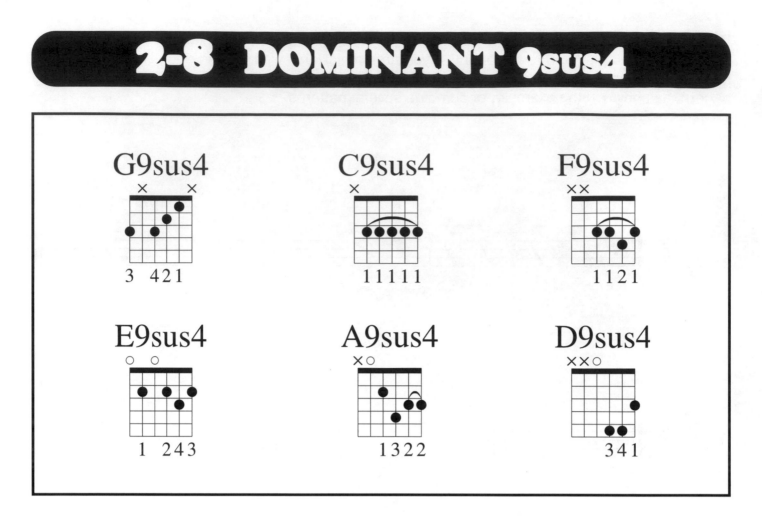

Here are six *dominant 9sus4* chords and three strumming patterns with more rests. As you recall, a *dot* following a note or rest increases its value by half. So, a dotted eighth rest in the first and third patterns below indicates a rest for **3/4 count**.

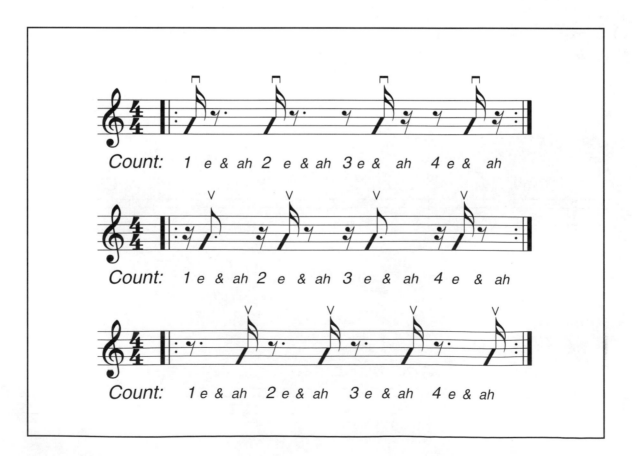

The dominant 9sus4 chords are often played in place of the dominant 7sus4 chords and used in such musical styles as funk, jazz, and contemporary pop. When you become comfortable with playing these chords and accompaniment patterns, move on to the following exercises. Use a metronome, count carefully, and try different strumming patterns for each progression.

Example:

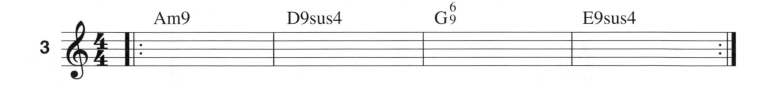

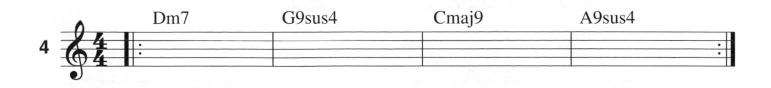

2-9 DOMINANT 7♭9

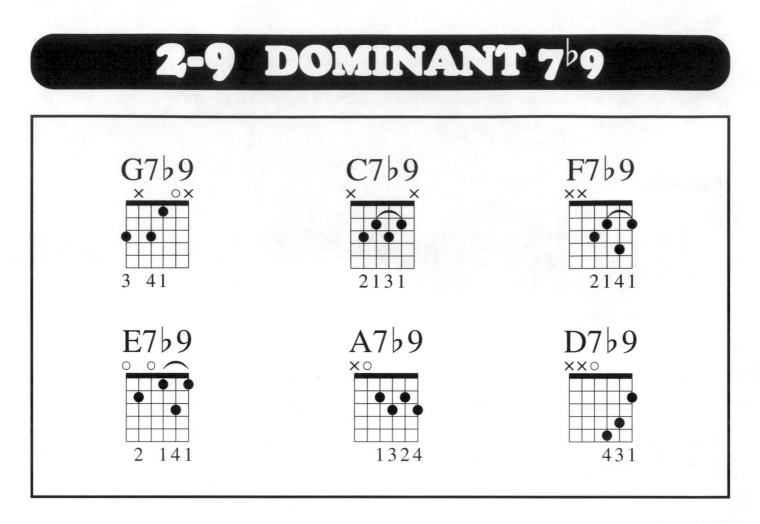

This section introduces *dominant 7♭9* chords. Notice the new time signature, *6/8*, in the accompaniment patterns. As explained on pages 12-13, 6/8 has two basic beats, each subdivided into three eighth notes, which is just like the triplet. At first, think of each click of the metronome as *one* eighth note and count **One-two-three-Four-five-six** per measure, slightly emphasizing **One** and **Four**.

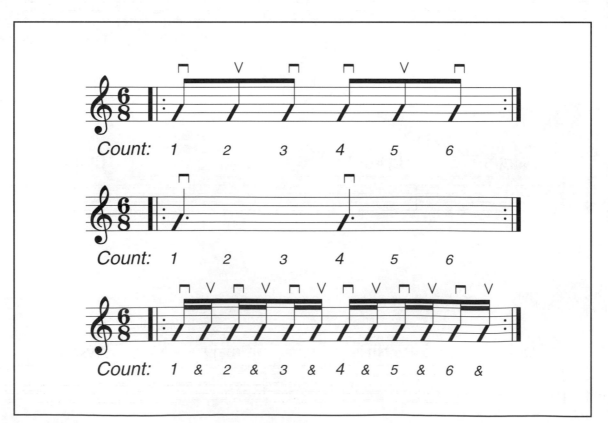

After you get used to playing in 6/8, set your metronome at a slower tempo. Regard each click as the basic beat and count ONE-TWO per measure, while mentally subdividing each click into three parts. When you are comfortable with the chords and 6/8 strumming patterns, practice the following chord progression exercises with a metronome.

Example:

1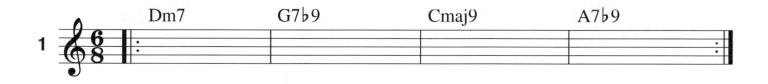

2

3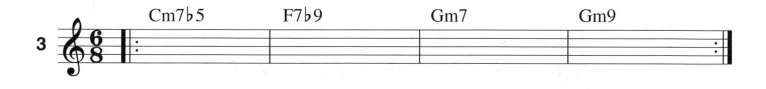

4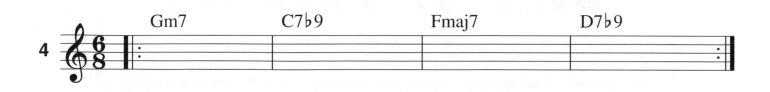

2-10 DOMINANT 7♯9

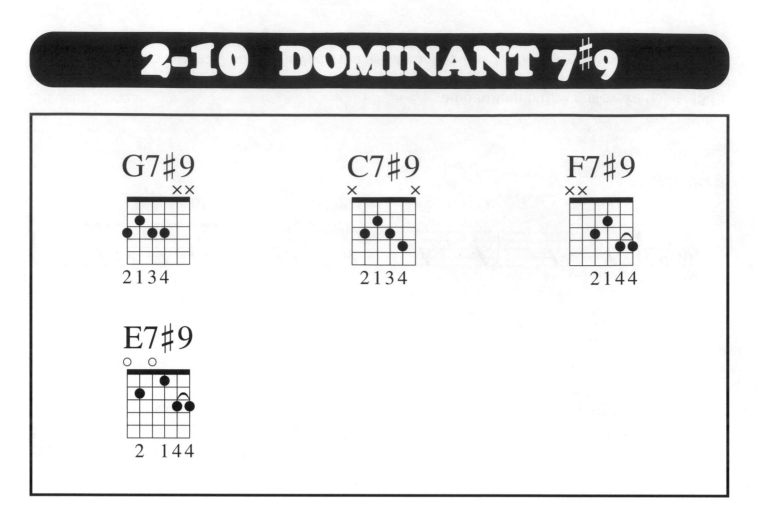

This last section of the chapter presents four *dominant 7♯9* chords and three strumming patterns in *12/8*. As you may notice, a measure of 12/8 is twice as long as a measure of 6/8. There are *four* basic beats, and each beat is again subdivided into three parts.

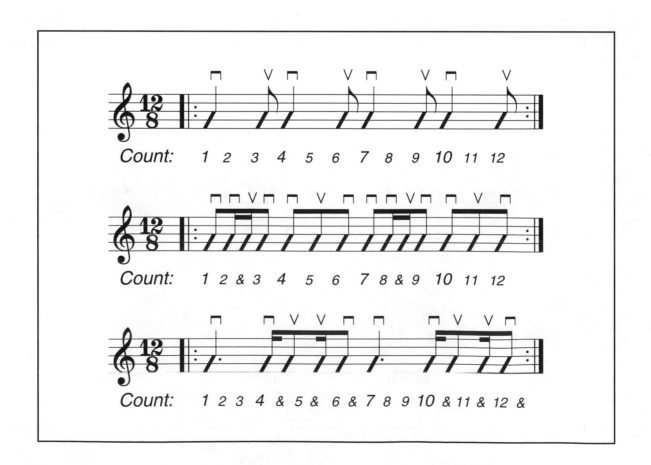

Along with the *shuffled-rhythm* patterns presented in Section 3-8 of *Guitar Chords and Accompaniment,* these accompaniment patterns are also used and played in many rock and blues songs. When practicing the first pattern, you can either alternate downstrokes and upstrokes as shown or play consecutive downstrokes. If you are comfortable with playing the new chords and accompaniment patterns, try the following exercises with a metronome.

Example:

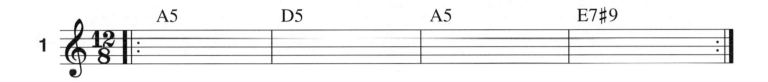

CHAPTER 2 REVIEW

The following exercises include some of the chords you have learned throughout this chapter. Review all the chords and strumming patterns first. Then, pick a pattern and play it throughout a chord progression or write out various accompaniments combining several patterns of your choice. Practice each exercise in different time signatures, 4/4, 3/4, 2/4, 6/8, and 12/8, with a metronome.

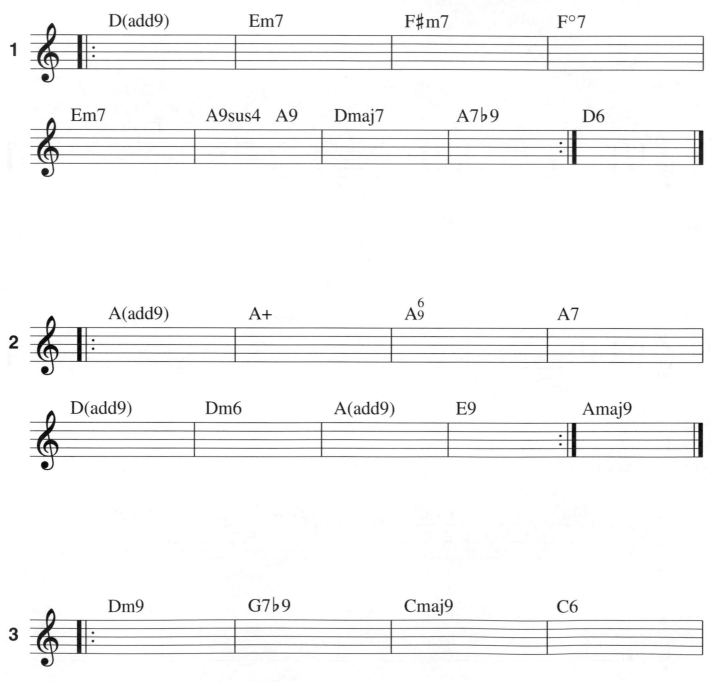

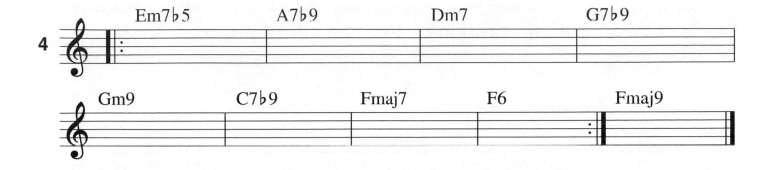

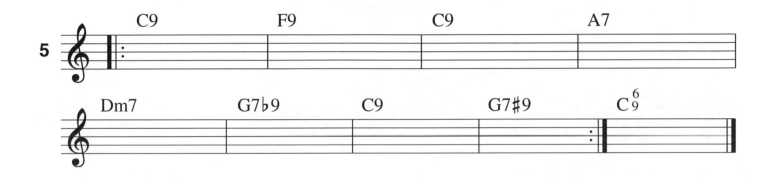

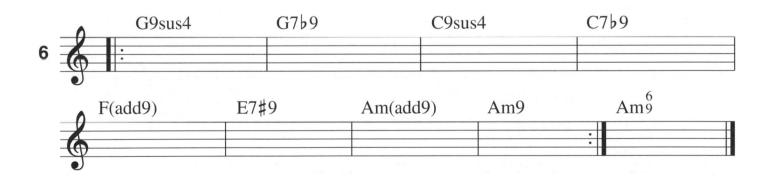

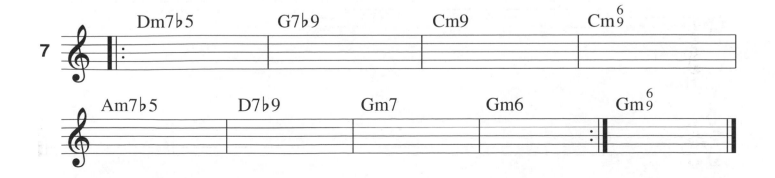

Write out and practice your own chord progressions.

CHAPTER 3
MORE CHORDS AND FINGERSTYLE

This chapter explores *fingerstyle* accompaniment patterns, again in various time signatures: 4/4, 3/4, 6/8, 3/8, 2/2, and 2/4. If you recall, fingerstyle—first introduced in Chapter 4 of *Guitar Chords and Accompaniment*—involves the use of your right-hand fingers instead of a pick. The patterns presented here, however, can also be played with a pick, and you are encouraged to try them with a pick or a combination of a pick and fingers. In this chapter, you will also learn six types of chords: *minor 11, dominant 11, dominant 13, major 7♭5, dominant 7♭5,* and *dominant 7♯5.* First, here is a brief review of the right-hand letters and TAB.

RIGHT-HAND LETTERS

The letters indicating the fingers of the right hand are shown below:

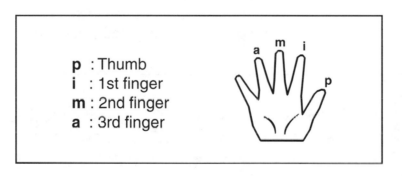

p : Thumb
i : 1st finger
m : 2nd finger
a : 3rd finger

TAB

A *tablature* or TAB is a six-line staff graphically showing the fingerboard. Each of the six lines represents a guitar string, as shown below. The numbers that appear on the lines are *fret* numbers indicating where to press down. *0* means open string, *1* means the 1st fret, and so on.

1st string
2nd string
3rd string
4th string
5th string
6th string

3-1 MINOR 11

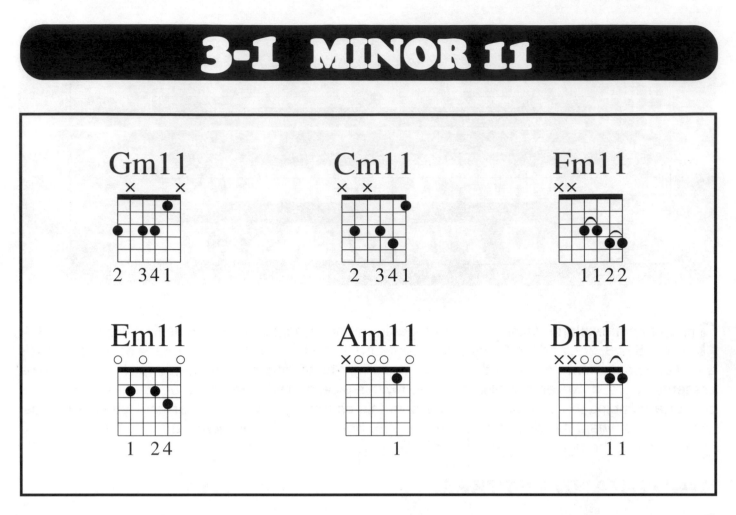

Sections 3-1 and 3-2 present six *fingerpicking* patterns not introduced in the previous book. As typically done in this style, the fingering indicates the exclusive use of three fingers: *p, i, m*. However, experiment with different fingerings and you may find something better suited to you.

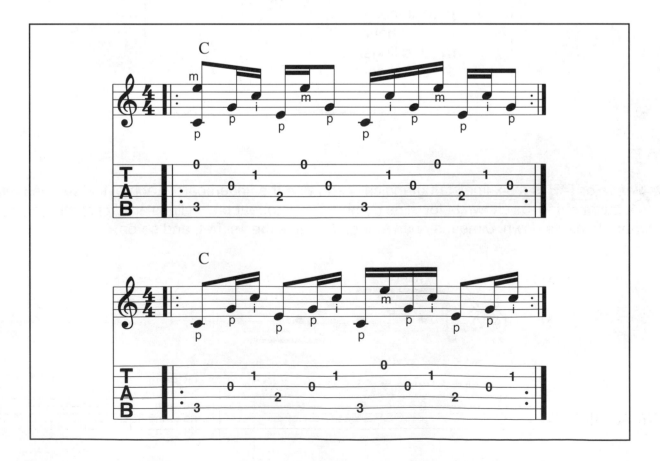

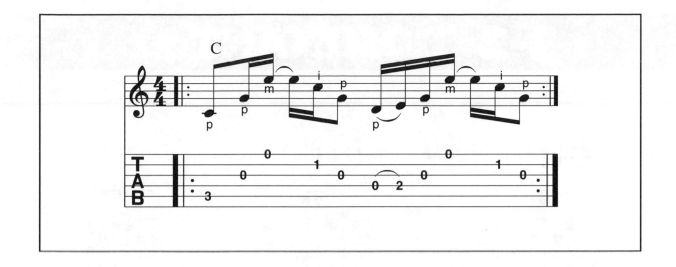

Notice the *hammer-on* used in the last pattern above. As done before, pick the first note, *D*, then hammer down on the 2nd fret of the 4th string with the left middle finger, without picking the string. Now, practice the following exercises with a metronome.

Example:

3-2 DOMINANT 11

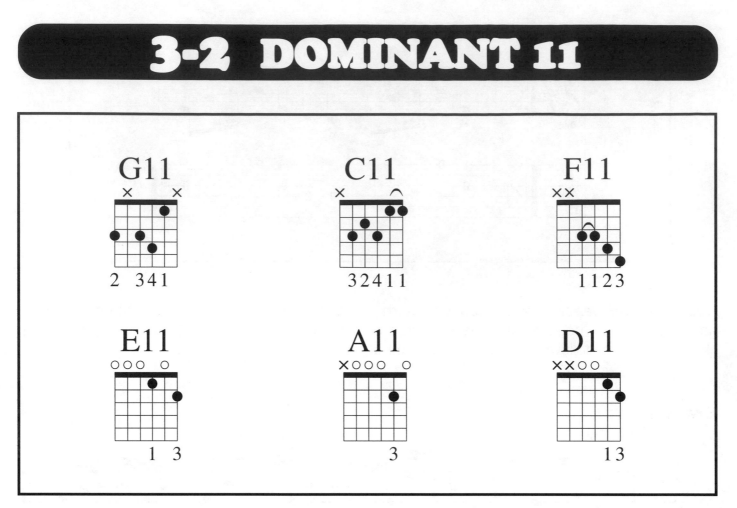

Here are six *dominant 11* chords and three fingerpicking patterns in 3/4. Many students tend to rush when playing these patterns, so be sure to use a metronome and play very *slowly* at first.

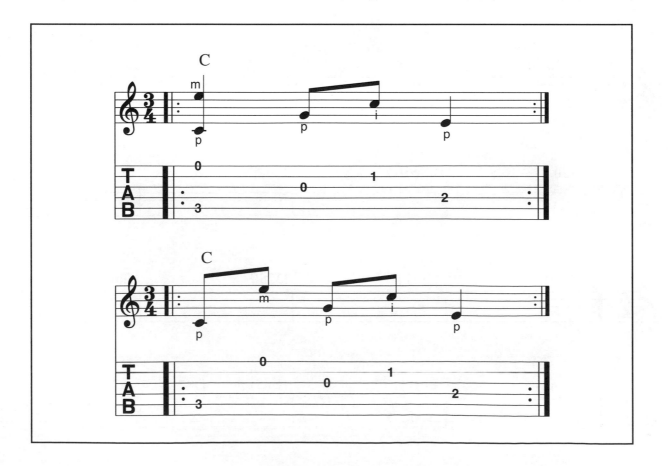

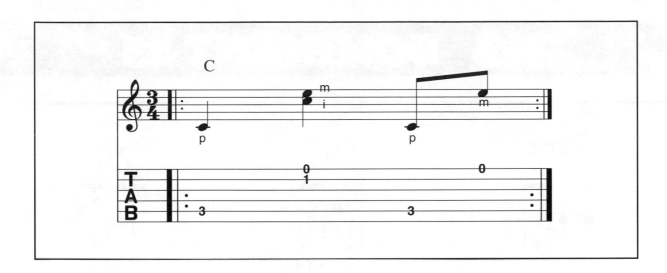

When you become comfortable with playing the above patterns, try the following exercises. As shown in the example, you can play throughout a progression using only one pattern or you can combine several patterns of your choice.

Example:

3-3 DOMINANT 13

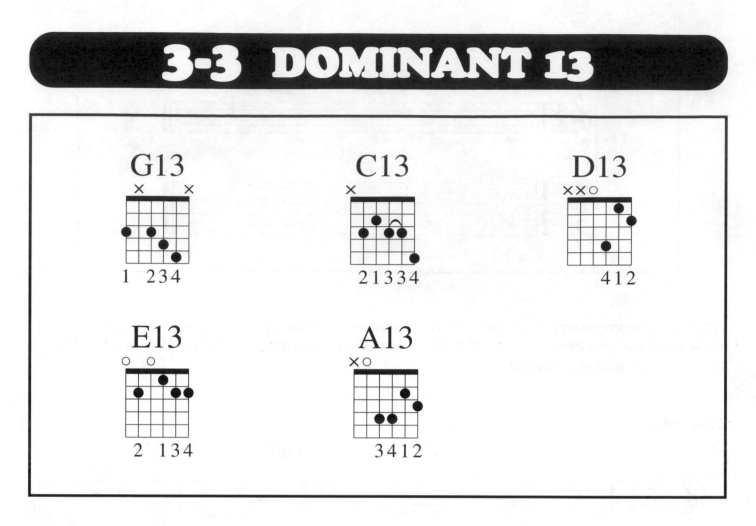

Here are five *dominant 13* chords and three *arpeggios* in 6/8. Arpeggios, as you may recall, are played by holding a chord and hitting one note after another in sequence. Each note should be played legato and held for its full value.

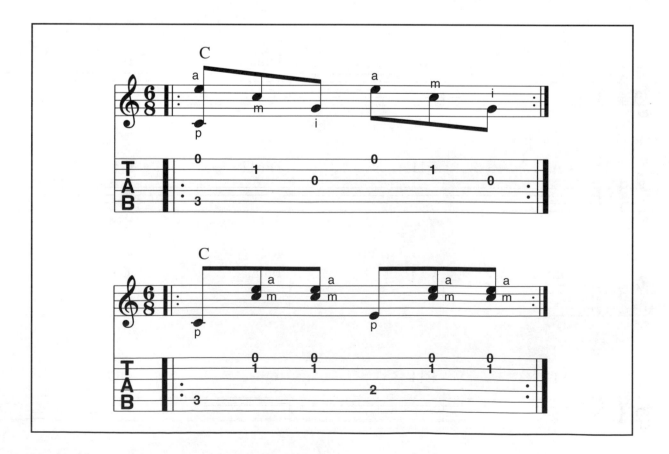

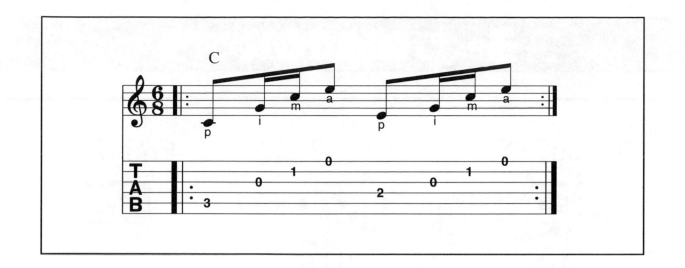

The *dominant 13* chords are very popular in jazz and Latin music. Study each diagram and follow the fingerings carefully. When you become comfortable with all of the chords and accompaniment patterns, move on to the following exercises.

Example:

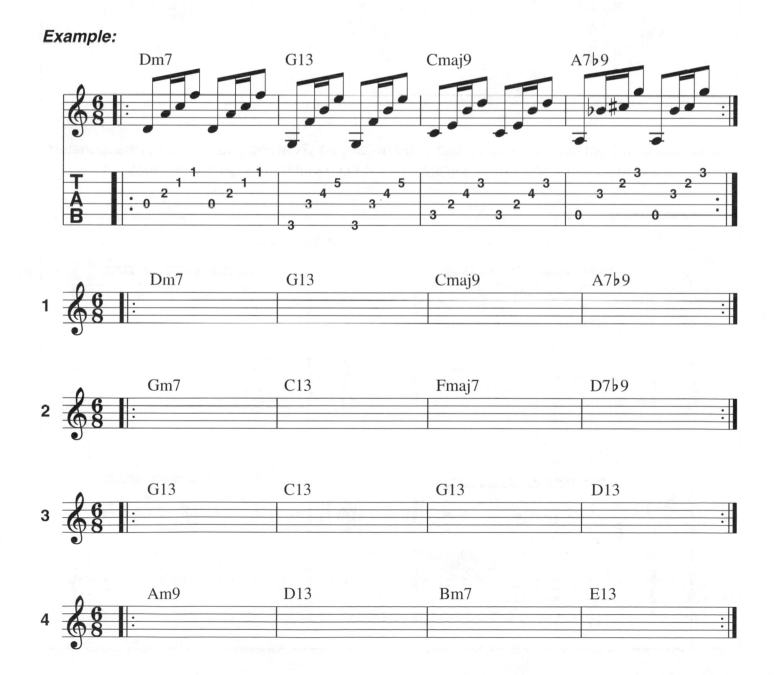

3-4 MAJOR 7♭5

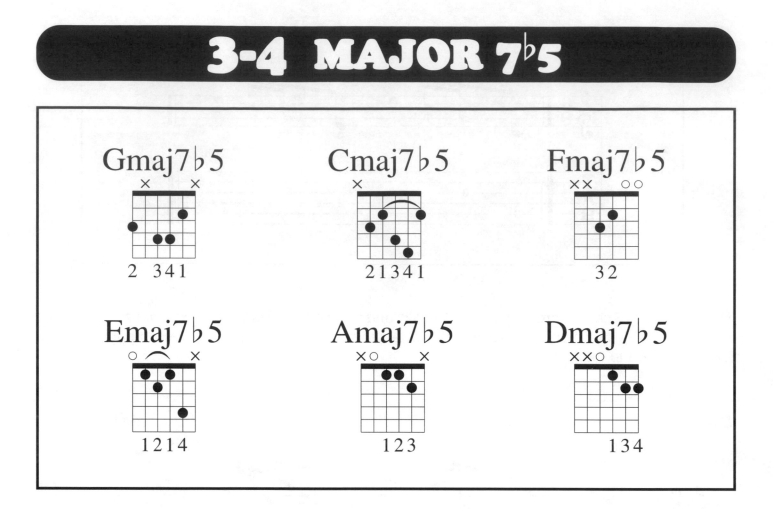

This section introduces you to six *major 7♭5* chords and six arpeggios in a new time signature, *3/8*. In 3/8, there are three counts per measure and an eighth note gets one count.

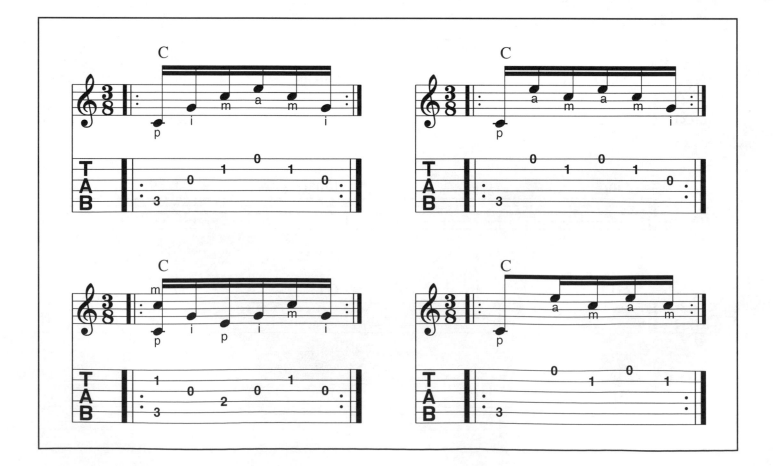

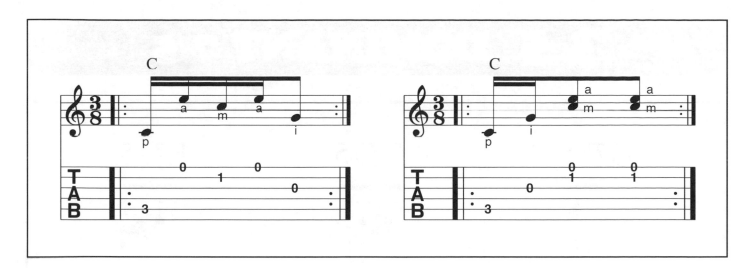

For the first pattern, subdivide each beat into two parts and count **1-&-2-&-3-&** while the metronome clicks on 1, 2, and 3. Count similarly for the other patterns. As in 3/4, put a slight accent on the first beat. Now, try the following chord progression exercises with a metronome.

Example:

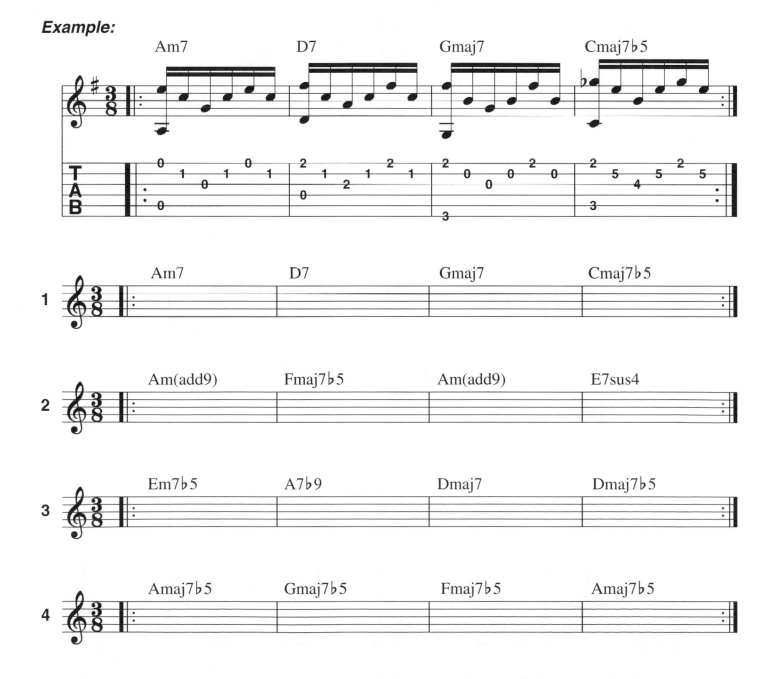

3-5 DOMINANT 7♭5

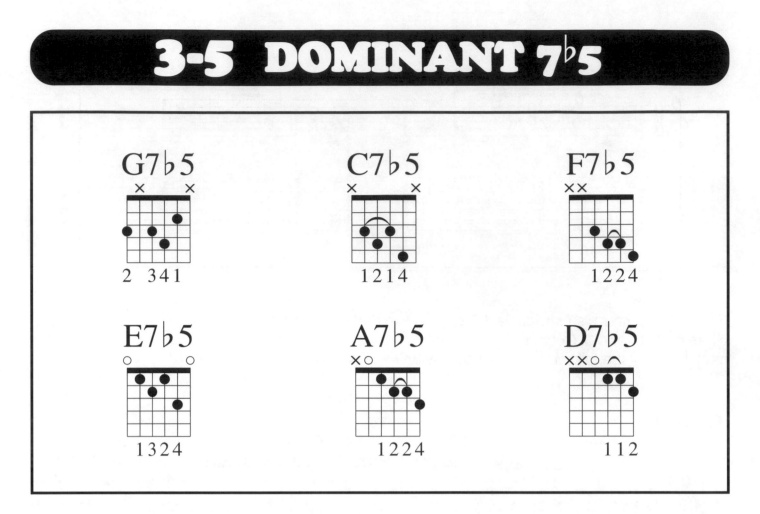

Here are six *dominant 7♭5* chords and some new accompaniment patterns in 2/2—or *cut time,* as it's sometimes called. In 2/2, there are two beats per measure and a half note gets one count. The symbol ¢ at the beginning of the staff is called *alla breve.* It's another common way to indicate 2/2.

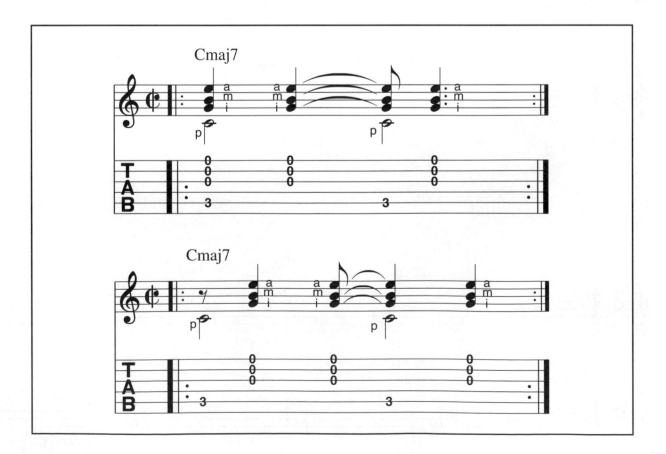

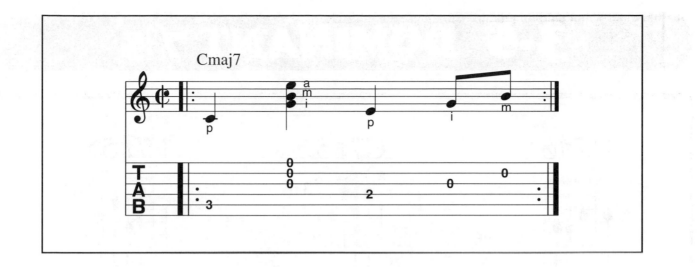

The first two patterns on the previous page are typically played in a popular Brazilian music style called *bossa nova*. If you have difficulty playing the upper and lower parts (chords and bass notes) together, isolate and play each part separately at first. Then put them together after you are comfortable with each.

Example:

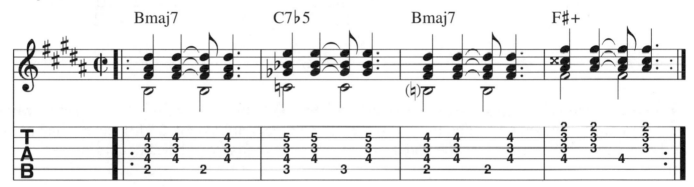

1

2

3

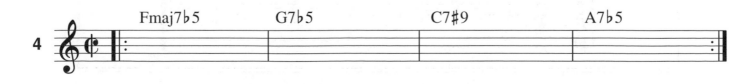

4

3-6 DOMINANT 7#5

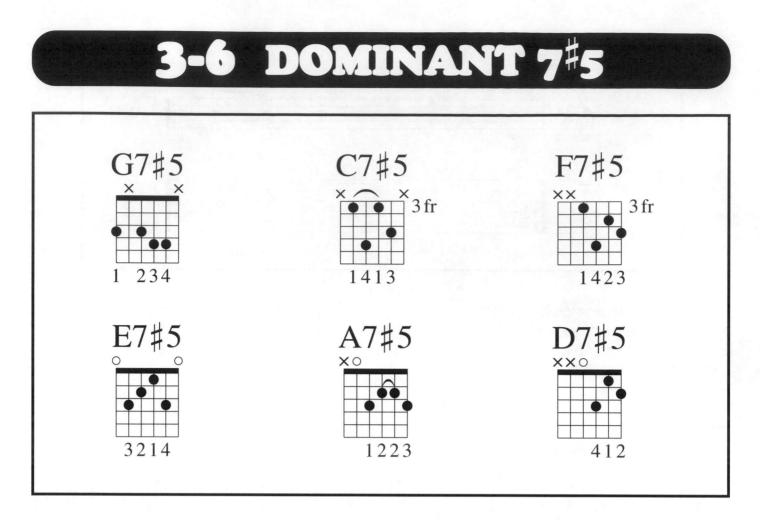

This last section presents six *dominant 7#5* chords and three fingerstyle patterns in *2/4,* where there are two beats per measure and a quarter note gets one count. So it's exactly half of 4/4, and how you count and play it is the same except that each measure has two counts instead of four.

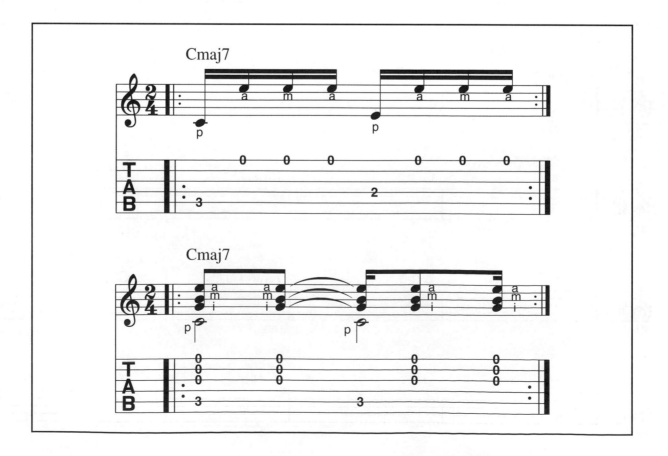

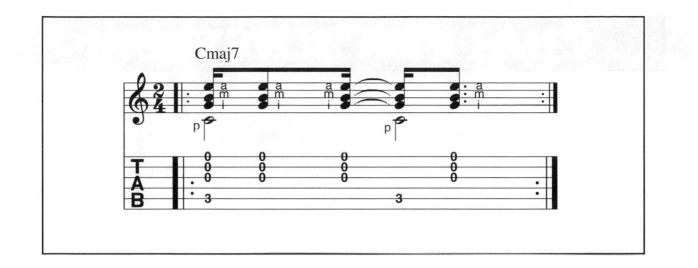

The fingering indicated in the first pattern (p-a-m-a) is one of five possible ways to play it. Try the other combinations as well: p-m-i-m, p-m-a-m, p-i-m-a, p-a-m-i. After you become comfortable with playing the chords and accompaniment patterns, try the exercises below.

Example:

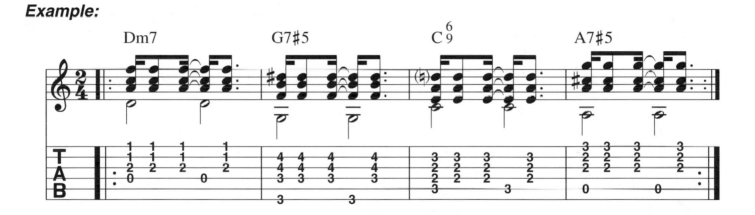

CHAPTER 3 REVIEW

First, review all the chords and fingerstyle patterns you've learned in this chapter. Then, as previously done, either pick a pattern and play it throughout a progression or combine several patterns of your choice and make up your own accompaniment. With a metronome, make sure you practice each exercise in various time signatures: 2/4, 4/4, 3/4, 3/8, 6/8, 12/8, 2/2.

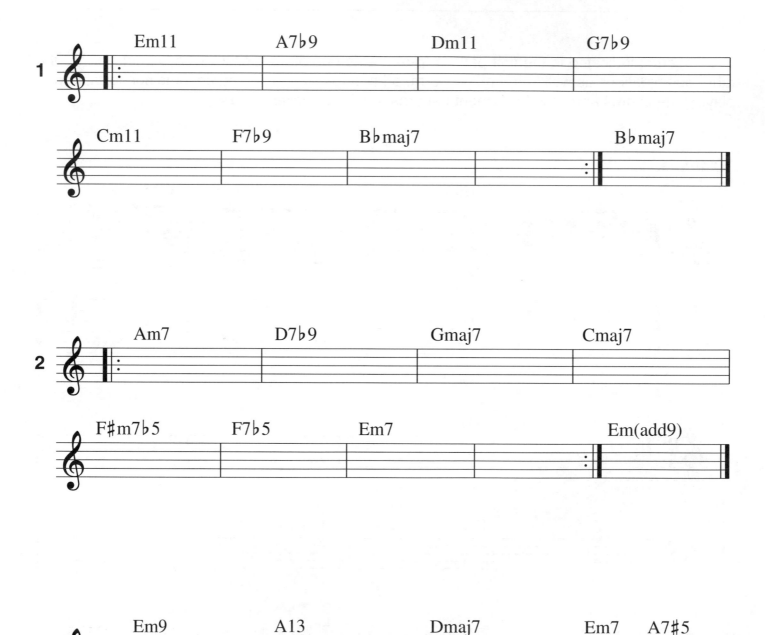

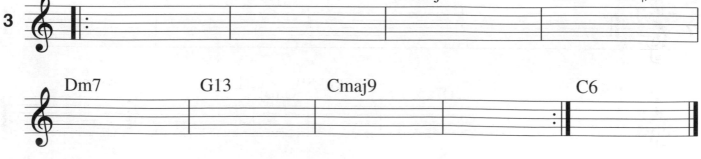

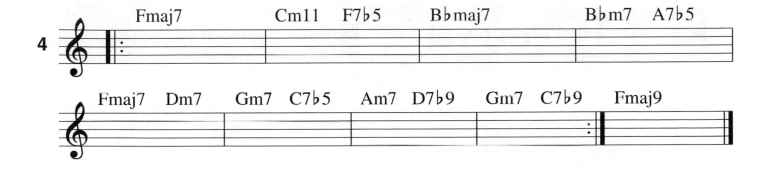

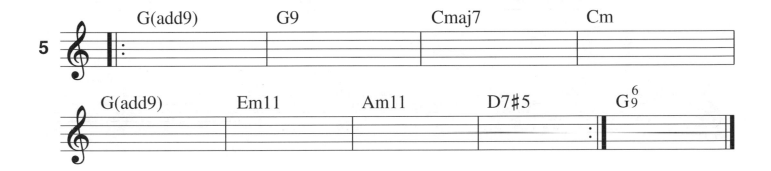

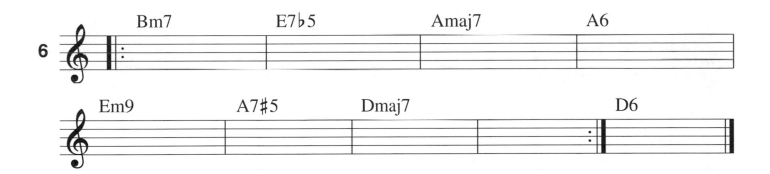

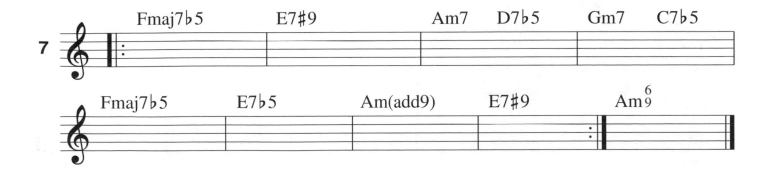

Write out and practice your own chord progressions.

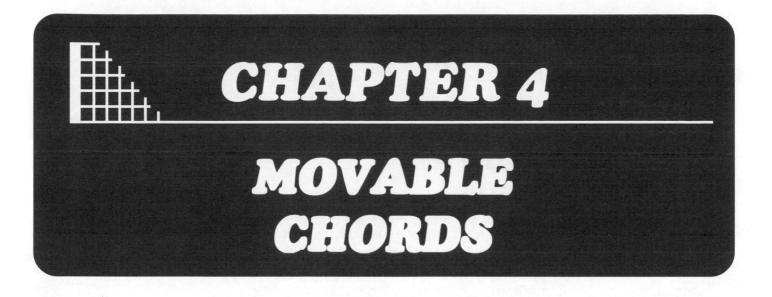

CHAPTER 4
MOVABLE CHORDS

In Chapter 3 of *Guitar Chords and Accompaniment*, you learned about *barre chords* and practiced transposing some of the open chords to different keys. Two chord forms you saw were *E-form*, which has a root on the 6th string, and *A-form* which has a root on the 5th string. You previously moved only six chords for each form, but virtually *any* chord can be moved by using the barre technique or the shifting techniques described below.

BARRE TECHNIQUE

You can move an open chord up and down the fingerboard by using your 1st finger as a *bar* across all six strings, in effect replacing the nut. As shown below, you create a barre chord by first holding an open chord with alternative fingering (E), then moving the chord shape up the fingerboard and laying your 1st finger across a fret, pressing on all six strings (F). You can play the chords of different roots simply by shifting the same chord shape to any other position on the fingerboard (G).

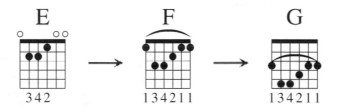

SHIFTING TECHNIQUES

Another way to transpose a chord to a different key is to simply *shift* it to an appropriate place using one of the following methods:

1. Shift Same Chord Shape

As an example, press C6 first. Then, without changing the chord shape or fingering, simply move it up one fret so that your 4th finger, which is pressing the root of the chord, will be on the 4th fret of the 5th string, as shown on the next page. As you may have already guessed, what you are now holding is a D♭6 chord. It is exactly the same chord shape as C6, but it's placed a half step up and hence the root of the chord is now D♭ instead of C. Notice when shifting the chord shape without using a barre, the open strings available to an open chord may sometimes not be playable in some of the chords with different roots. For example, the open 1st string played in C6 is not part of the D♭6 chord and therefore should be muted, along with the 6th string, or you will hear some dissonance.

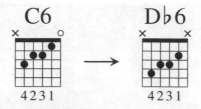

2. Root Added by 1st Finger

As an alternative to the barre technique, you can shift a chord to a different position on the fingerboard by simply adjusting the basic fingering and adding the root with your 1st finger instead of barring all six strings. For instance, play Amaj7 with your 2nd, 3rd, and 4th fingers as shown below. Then shift the same chord shape up one fret and, instead of pressing all six strings at the 1st fret, simply press the 1st fret of the 5th string, or B♭, with your 1st finger. The result is a simpler way to play B♭maj7 without an extended barre.

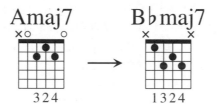

3. Altered Voicing

When the chord you are holding uses all four fingers, you need to alter the chord shape or voicing slightly so that you can move it up or down and press the new root. For instance, when transposing E6 up a half step, you need to change the voicing, as shown in the middle diagram below, to free your 1st finger and allow it to press the root of F6, the F note.

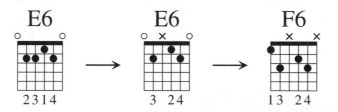

4. Assumed Root

As an alternative to the above method, when you are using all four fingers, you can simply shift the chord without changing the fingering or even playing the new root. Instead, you move the same chord shape along with fingerboard and *assume* where the root of the new chord is. The gray dot below (●) indicates the root of F6, or the F note that is not being pressed but is simply assumed.

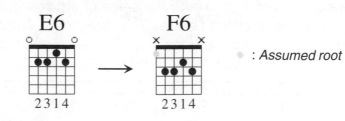

● : *Assumed root*

4-1 ROOTS ON THE 6TH STRING

In Section 4-1, you'll study chords that have roots on the 6th string. *Guitar Chords and Accompaniment* presented six *E-form* movable chords based on the open chords: E, E7, Em, Em7, Esus4, and E7sus4. However, all chords with **E** as their root—such as Emaj7, E(add9), E9, etc.—can be considered E-form, and they are transposable to different roots as well. Another shape that has roots on the 6th string and can be similarly moved along the fingerboard is *G-form,* which is based on G chords such as G, Gmaj7, G7, G9, etc. Before proceeding, review the names of notes on the 6th string using the fingerboard diagrams with music notation and TAB below.

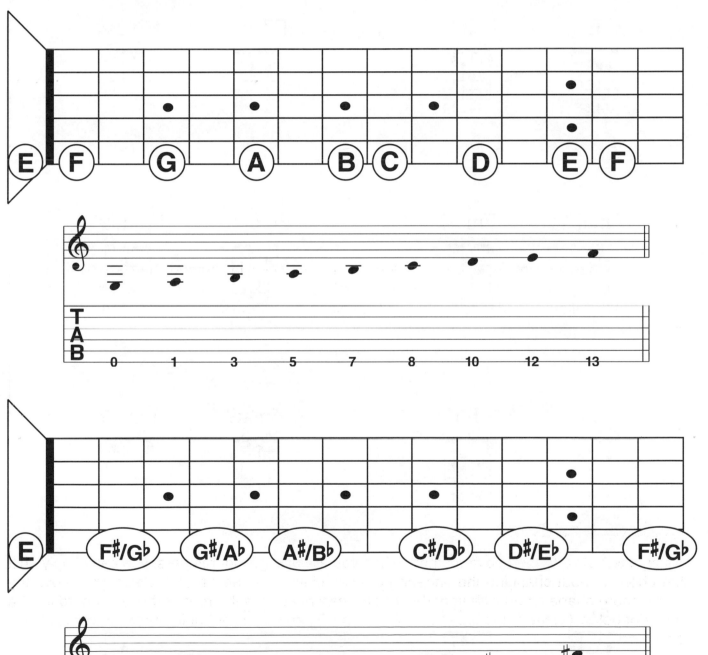

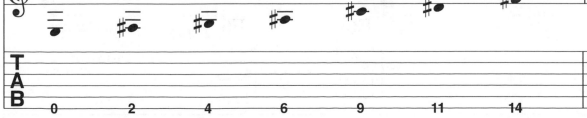

E-FORM MOVABLE CHORDS

E-form movable chords include all chords that have an **E** note as their root, such as E, E5, Em, E7, E9sus4, etc. As indicated in the examples below, practice moving various E-form chords along the fingerboard using the barre or shifting techniques.

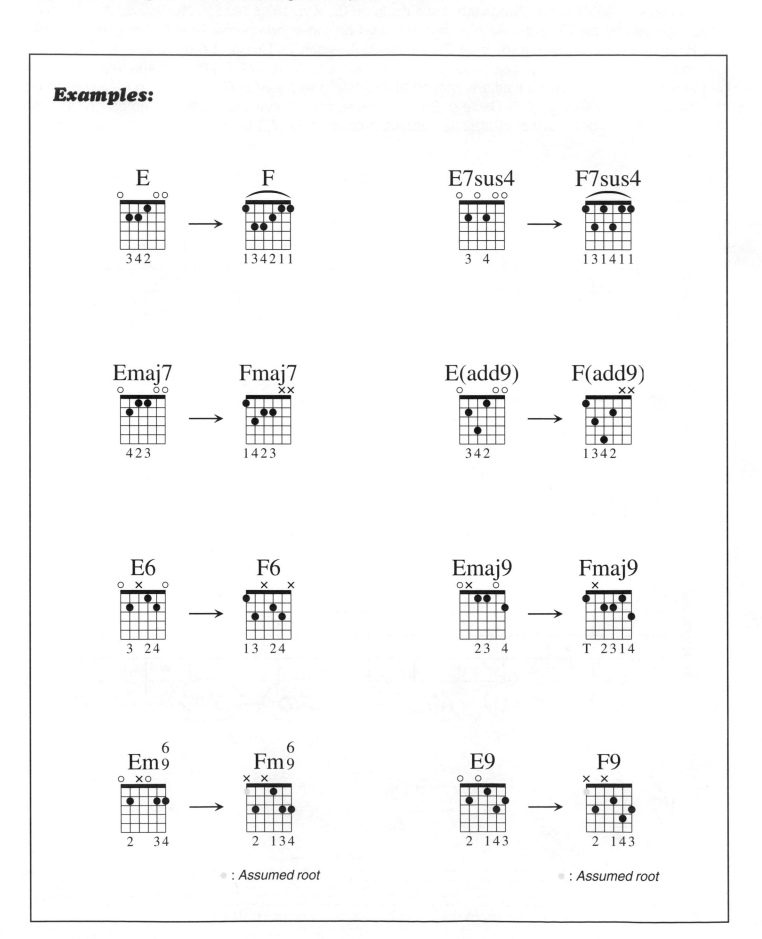

Examples:

Using the chord progressions below, practice moving the E-form movable chords. In the first exercise, you will move the Emaj7 chord through all 12 keys. Be sure to practice all the other types of E-form movable chords as well. Write out an accompaniment and practice with a metronome.

1 Practice all of the E-form movable chords: *E, E5, E6, E6/9, Esus2, Esus4, E(add9), Emaj7, Emaj9, Emaj7♭5, Em, Em7, Em7♭5, Em(maj7), Em6, Em(add9), Em6/9, Em9, Em11, E7, E7sus4, E9sus4, E9, E11, E13, E7♭5, E7♯5, E7♭9, E7♯9, E°7, E+.*

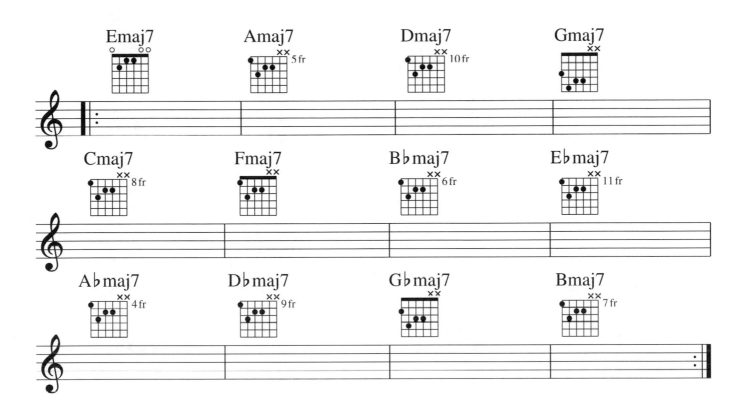

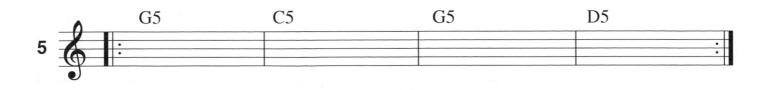

G-FORM MOVABLE CHORDS

G-form movable chords have a **G** note as their root. They include such chords as: G, Gmaj9, Gmaj7♭5, G7, G°7, etc. Study the examples below and practice moving the G-form chords to various roots along the fingerboard.

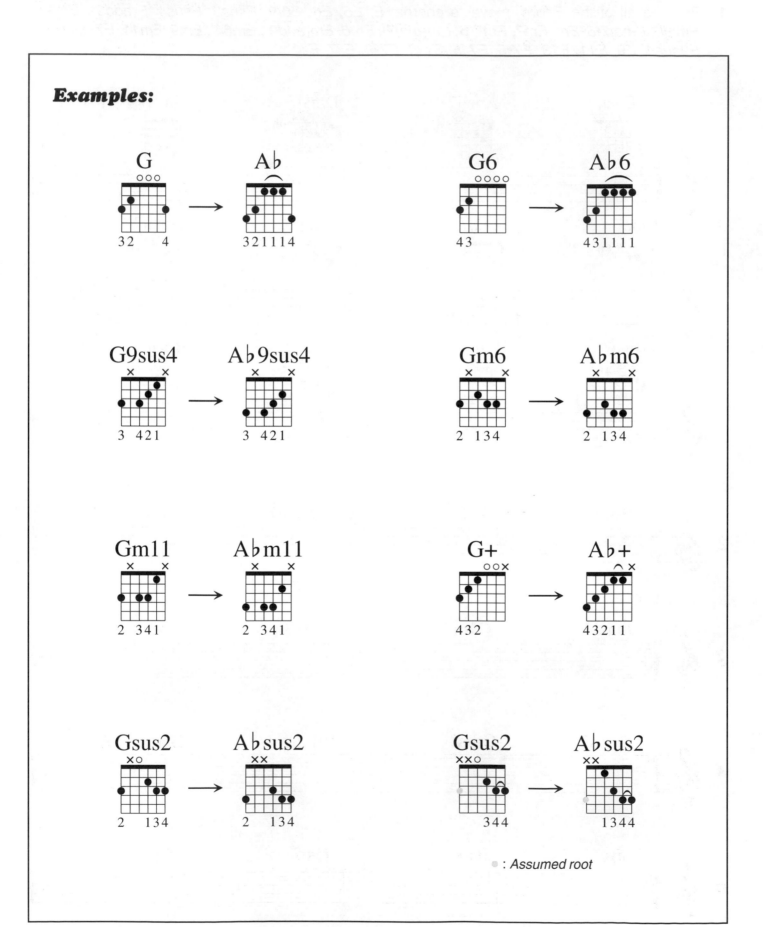

● : *Assumed root*

Using the chord progressions below, practice moving the G-form movable chords. In exercise #1, you will move the G6 chord through all 12 keys. Be sure to practice all the other types of G-form movable chords as well. Write out an accompaniment and play it with a metronome.

1 Practice all of the G-form movable chords: *G, G5, G6, G6/9, Gsus2, Gsus4, G(add9), Gmaj7, Gmaj9, Gmaj7♭5, Gm7♭5, Gm(add9), Gm6/9, Gm11, G7, G7sus4, G9, G9sus4, G11, G13, G7♭5, G7♯5, G7♭9, G7♯9, G°7, G+.*

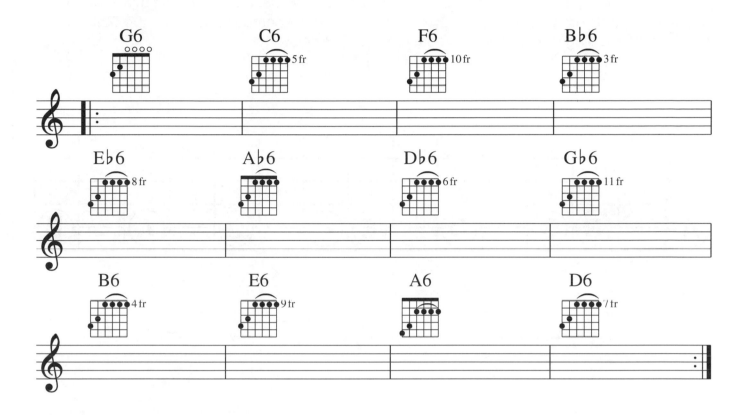

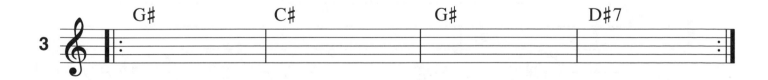

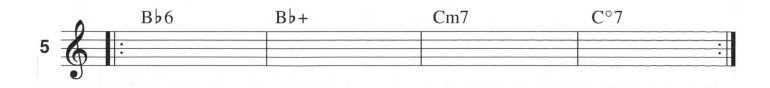

4-2 ROOTS ON THE 5TH STRING

There are two forms of movable chords whose roots are on the 5th string: *A-form* and *C-form*. The introductory book presented six A-form chords based on A, A7, Am, Am7, Asus4, and A7sus4. However, similar to E-form movable chords, *all* chords with **A** as their root are considered A-form and movable. Likewise, chords based on C—such as C6, Cmaj9, C9, etc.—can also be moved along the fingerboard to different roots. Before proceeding, review the names of notes on the 5th string using the fingerboard diagrams with music notation and TAB below.

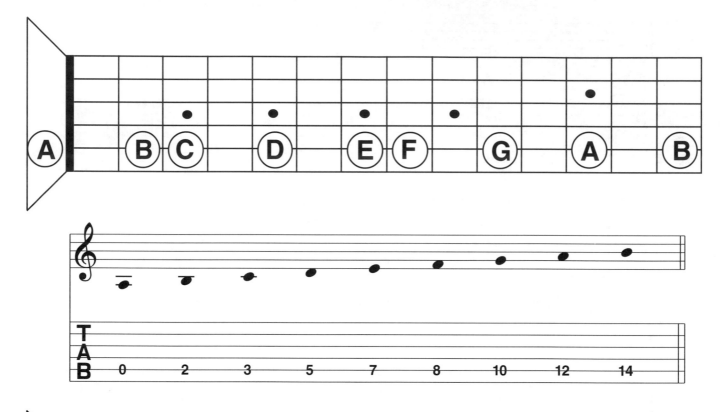

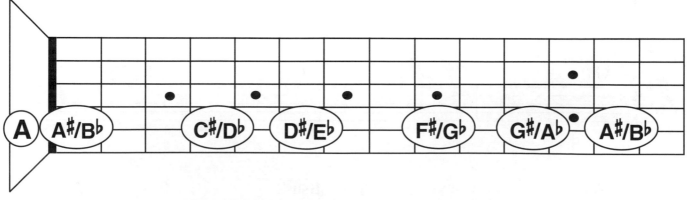

A-FORM MOVABLE CHORDS

A-form movable chords have an **A** note as their root and include such chords as A, Amaj7, Am7, A7, A7♭9, etc. As indicated below in the examples, practice moving all of the other A-form chords to different places on the fingerboard.

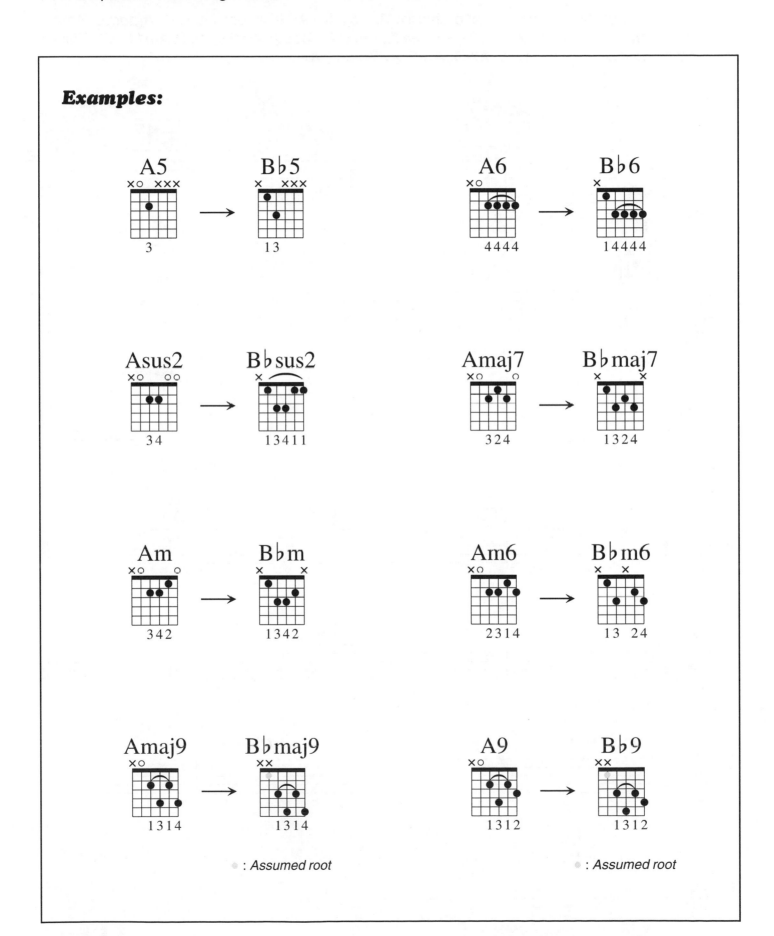

Using the chord progressions below, practice moving the A-form movable chords. Notice that exercise #1 shows how you can move a dominant 9 chord along the fingerboard while *assuming* the root and without changing the shape. Practice all of the other A-form chords in a similar fashion.

1 Practice all of the A-form movable chords: *A, A5, A6, A6/9, Asus2, Asus4, A(add9), Amaj7, Amaj9, Amaj7♭5, Am, Am7, Am7♭5, Am(maj7), Am6, Am(add9), Am6/9, Am9, Am11, A7, A7sus4, A9, A9sus4, A11, A13, A7♭5, A7♯5, A7♭9, A7♯9, A°7, A+.*

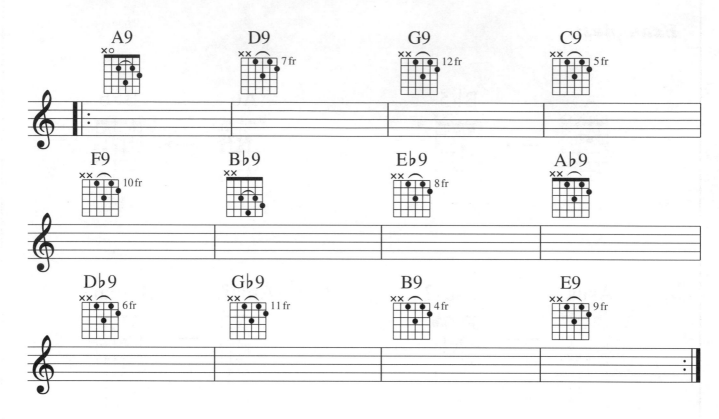

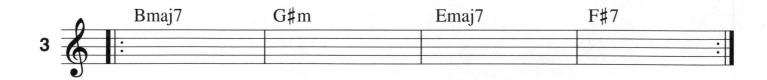

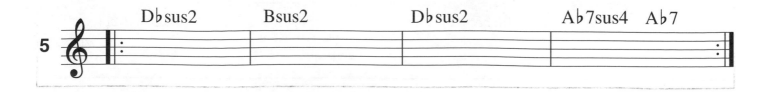

C-FORM MOVABLE CHORDS

C-form movable chords have a **C** note as their root and include such chords as C, C7, Cm7, C7sus4, Cmaj7, etc. Below you will find various examples that demonstrate how you can move C-form chords to a different root. In a similar fashion, practice all of the other chord forms.

Examples:

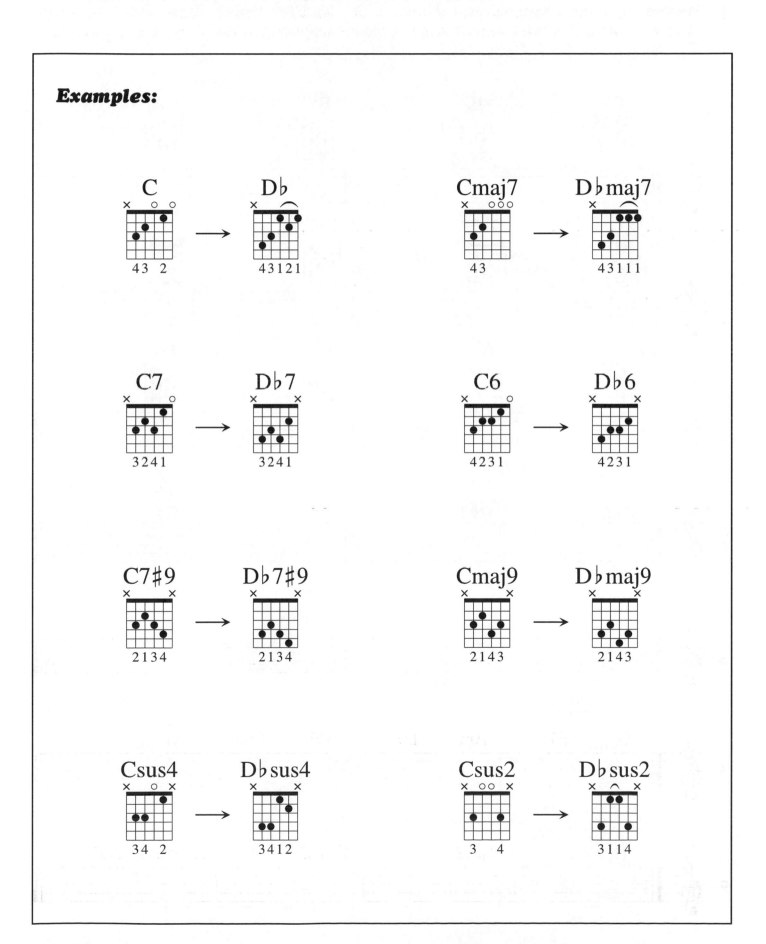

Using the chord progression exercises below, practice moving the C-form movable chords. As indicated in exercise #1, practice moving each C-form movable chord through all 12 keys. Make up an accompaniment or two and play it with a metronome.

1 Practice all of the C-form movable chords: *C, C5, C6, C6/9, Csus2, Csus4, C(add9), Cmaj7, Cmaj9, Cmaj7♭5, Cm7♭5, Cm6, Cm(add9), Cm6/9, Cm9, Cm11, C7, C7sus4, C9, C9sus4, C11, C13, C7♭5, C7♯5, C7♭9, C7♯9, C°7, C+.*

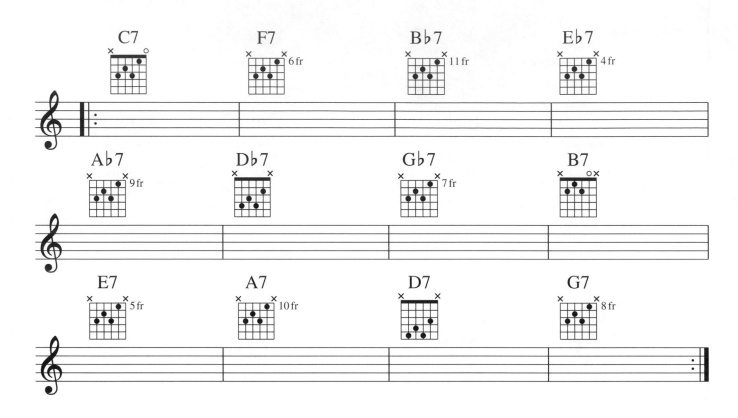

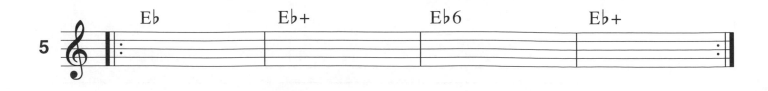

4-3 ROOTS ON THE 4TH STRING

By this time, you may have wondered, "Are the chords whose roots are on the 6th and 5th strings the only ones that are movable? What about those open chords whose roots are on the 4th string, such as D, Dm, Dm7, etc.? Aren't they movable as well?" You've guessed it right. All those chords whose roots are on the 4th string are also movable, and next you'll look at two of those forms: *D-form* and *F-form*. Before moving ahead, study the names of notes that are on the 4th string with the help of the fingerboard diagrams and music notation and TAB below.

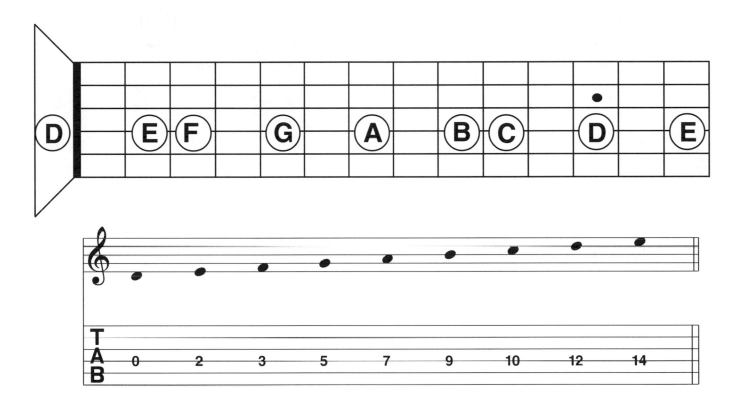

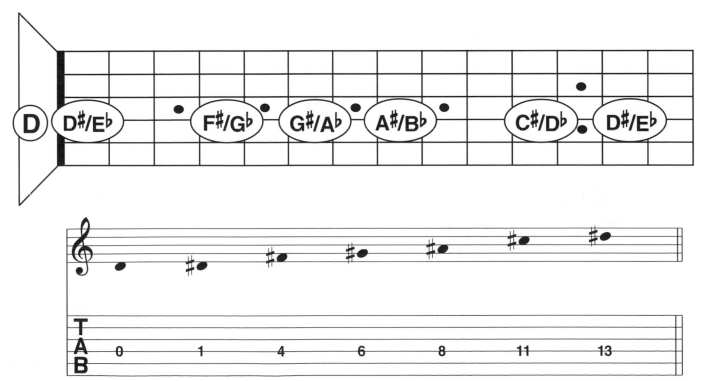

D-FORM MOVABLE CHORDS

The first movable form that has the root on the 4th string is *D-form*. All D-form movable chords have a **D** note as their root, and they include D, Dm7, D9, Dmaj7, etc. Here are some examples that show you how to move D-form chords.

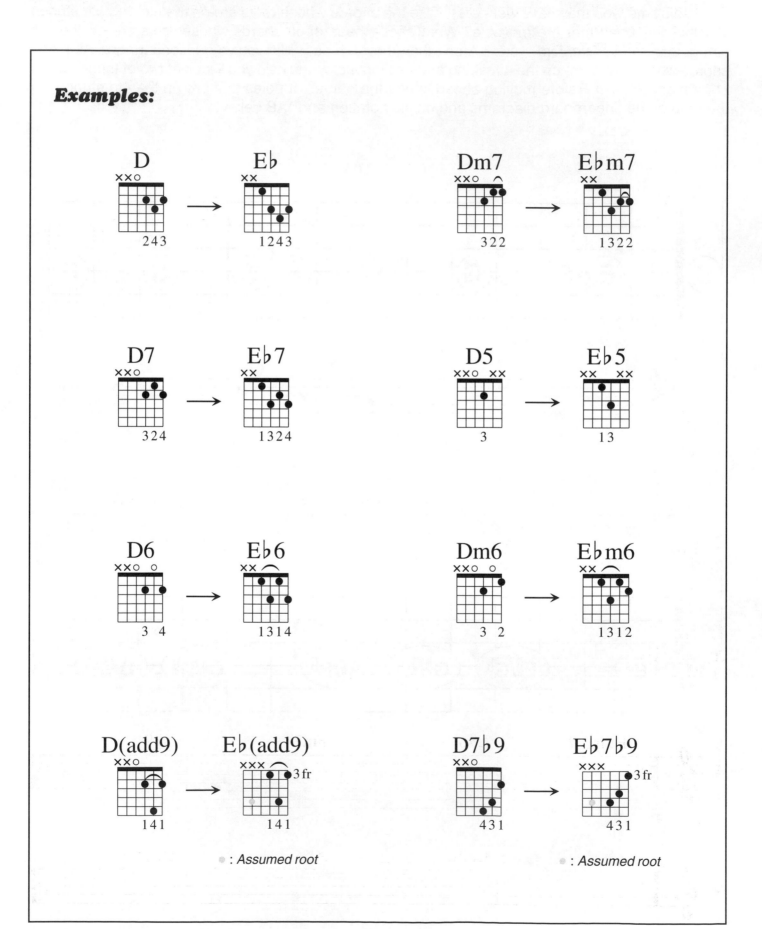

Using the chord progression exercises below, practice moving the D-form movable chords. As indicated in exercise #1, be sure to practice moving all of the D-form chords through all 12 keys. Also, add an accompaniment or two and play it with a metronome.

1 Practice all of the D-form movable chords: *D, D5, D6, Dsus2, Dsus4, D(add9), Dmaj7, Dmaj7♭5, Dm, Dm7, Dm7♭5, Dm(maj7), Dm6, Dm(add9), Dm11, D7, D7sus4, D9sus4, D11, D13, D7♭5, D7♯5, D7♭9, D°7, D+.*

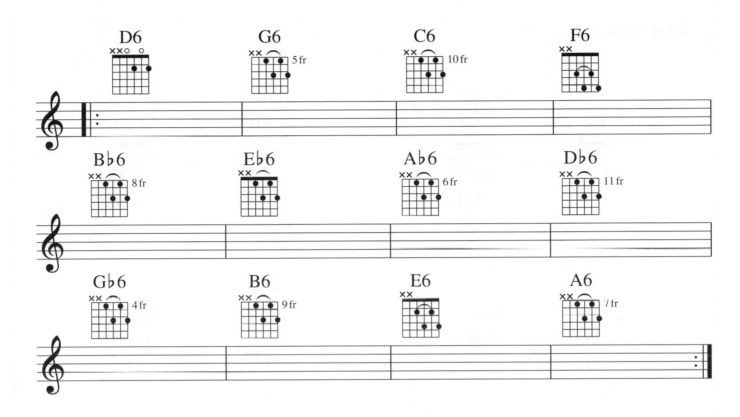

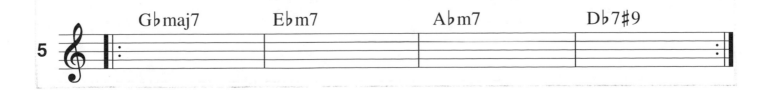

F-FORM MOVABLE CHORDS

The last movable form is *F-form* which has an **F** note as the root. Such chords as Fmaj7, F6, F5, and Fm9 are some examples. Study some of the ways you can transpose F-form movable chords along the fingerboard as shown in the examples below.

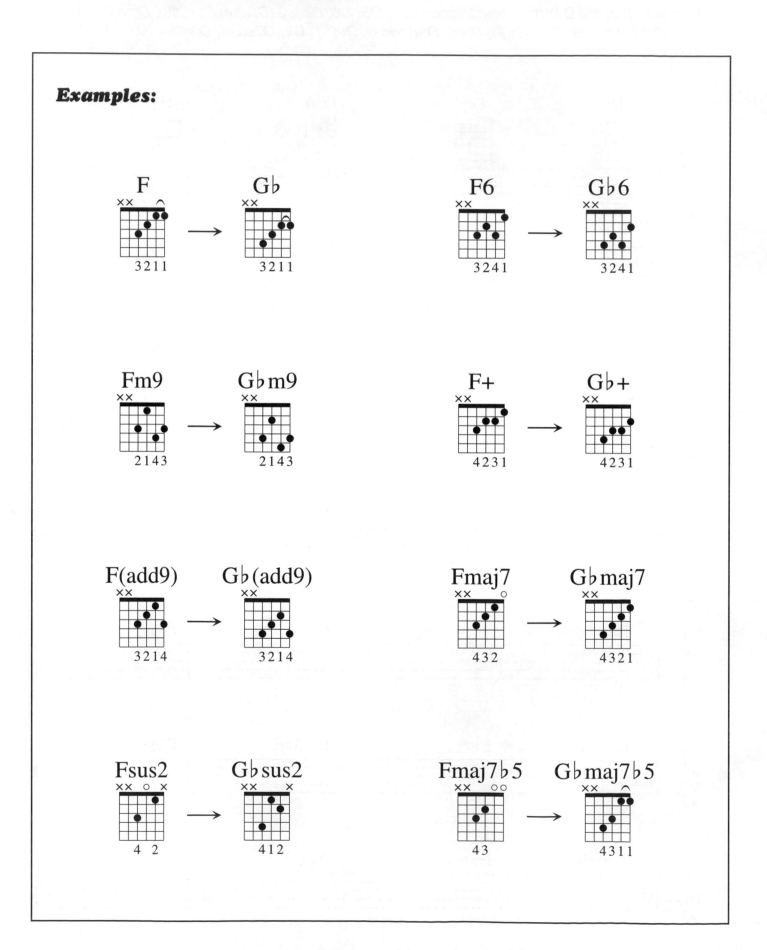

Practice moving the F-form movable chords using the chord progression exercises below. As indicated in exercise #1, take each F-form chord and play it in all 12 keys by shifting it to the appropriate places. Don't forget to create an accompaniment and play it with a metronome.

1 Practice all of the F-form movable chords: *F, F5, F6, F6/9, Fsus2, Fsus4, F(add9), Fmaj7, Fmaj9, Fmaj7♭5, Fm, Fm7♭5, Fm6, Fm(add9), Fm9, Fm11, F7, F7sus4, F9sus4, F11, F7♭5, F7♯5, F7♭9, F°7, F+.*

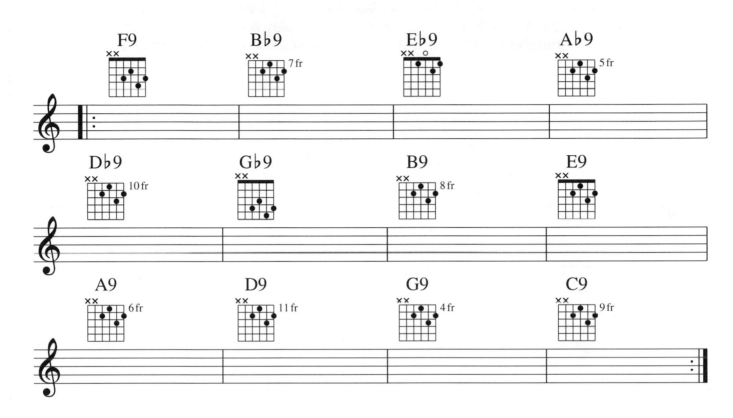

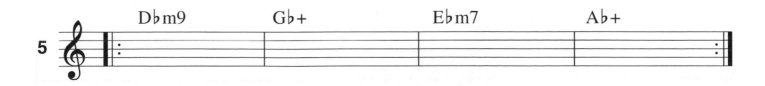

CHAPTER 4 REVIEW

As you may have already noticed, there is more than one way to play a chord and each exercise by combining different movable chord forms. For practice, try setting some arbitrary range of positions within which to stay and play an exercise instead of jumping around the fingerboard. For example, one possible way to play exercise #1 below is to stay between open and the 5th fret while mixing various movable forms. In general, the closer you play a chord to another, the easier and smoother the chord transition will be. Now practice each exercise in different time signatures with a metronome.

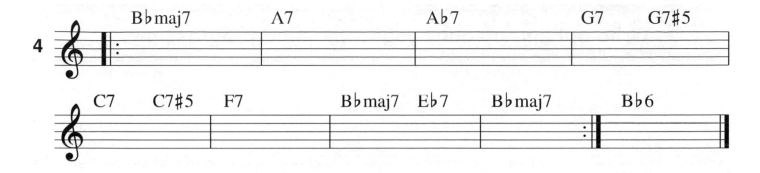

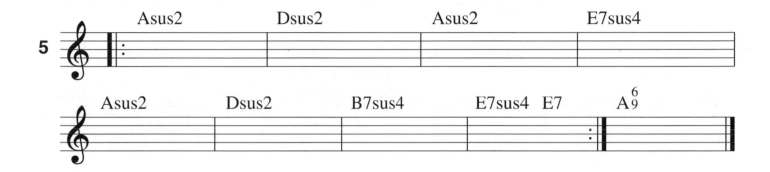

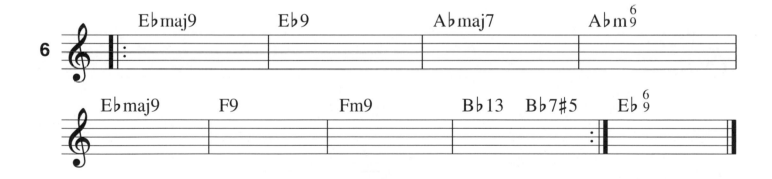

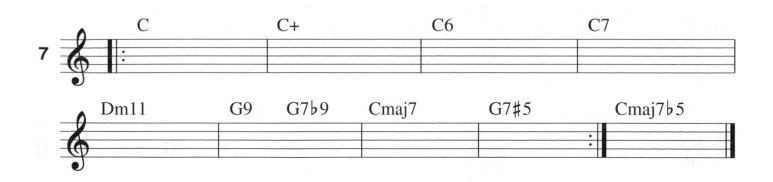

Write out and practice your own chord progressions.

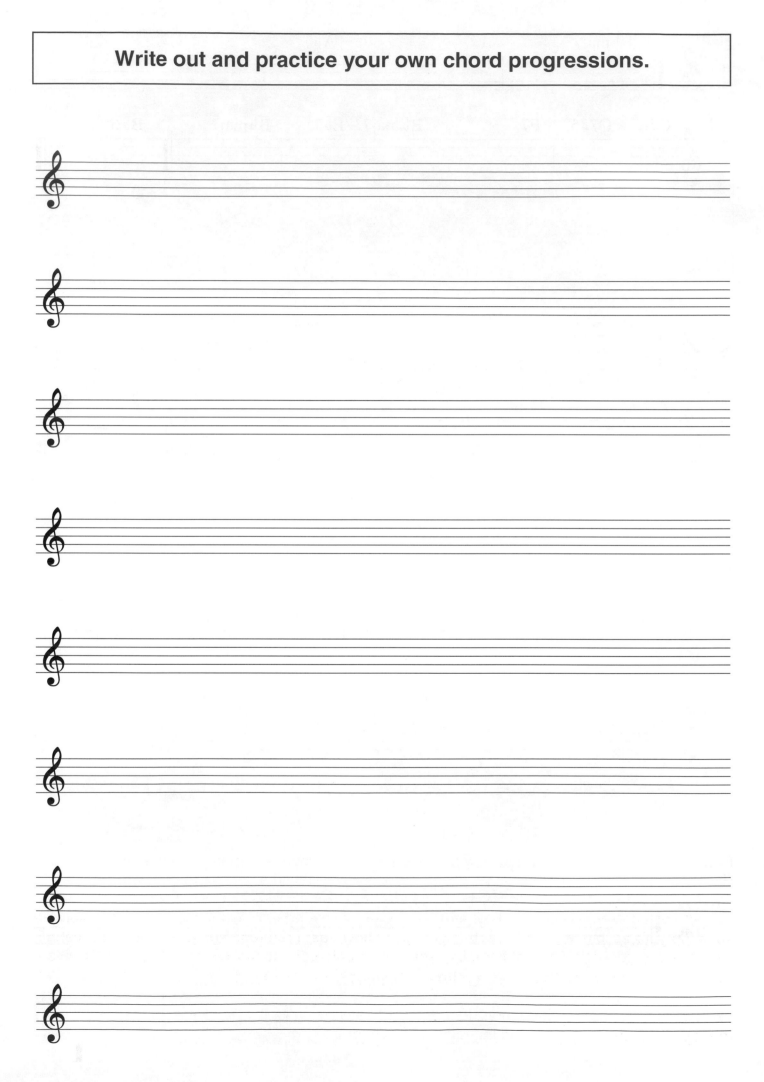

CHAPTER 5

ALTERNATIVE CHORD FORMS

Each chord form shown in the introductory book and in the first two chapters of this book is only one of many possible ways you can play the chord on the guitar. By rearranging one note or more notes of a chord, it can be played in a number of different ways and positions. In fact, you have already seen variations of a chord in your study of the barre and movable chords. For instance, from applying various forms of movable chords, you realize that you already know six ways to play the C chord:

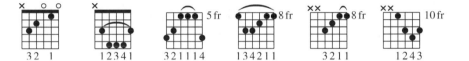

On the following pages, you will find charts of selected *alternative chord forms* for many of the open and slash chords. On page 78, for example, you will see eleven other ways to play the familiar open C chord, six ways to play C/E, etc. Which chord form you choose to play depends on several factors, including:

- What particular sound you are seeking or hearing in your head at the moment.
- How the chord will sound within the song context or chord progression you are playing.
- Whether it's physically easy or difficult to play or to make a smooth chord connection.
- The type and arrangement of the particular tune.

Play each chord form, observing how it differs and how it sounds compared to the original shape. Experiment with various other ways, select or create your favorite versions, and organize them in your own fashion. Don't feel overwhelmed by all the variations! Regard these charts as a reference that you can come back to from time to time whenever you are looking for a new sound or need to spice up your accompaniment. Each fingering is shown as a reference only. Sometimes a certain situation may call for a different fingering—for example, in order to make a smooth chord transition. You are encouraged to try different fingerings and find the ones you are most comfortable with. Lastly, all chords are written in the key of C. However, they are all *movable*—which means that you can transpose and play each chord form in all 12 keys by using the *barre* and *shifting* techniques (pages 57-58) that you practiced in the previous chapter.

5-1 ALTERNATIVE MAJOR CHORD FORMS

C

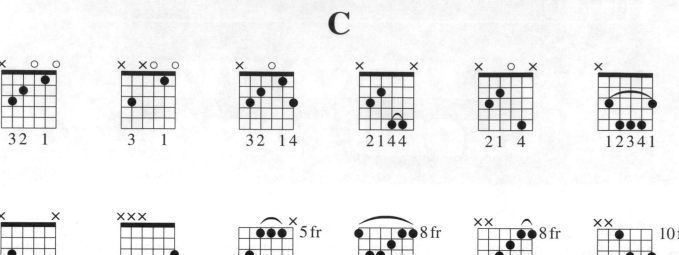

C/E

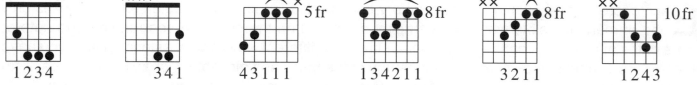

C/G

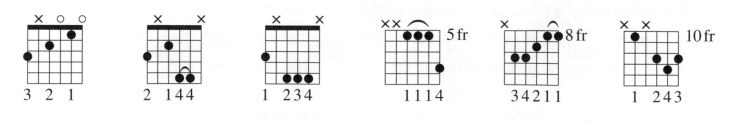

C/B

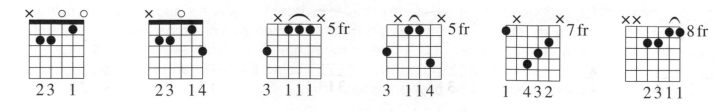

C6

 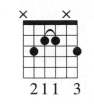 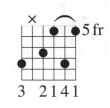 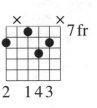 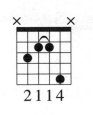 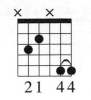

4231 2 1 1 3 2 1 1 4 2 1 4 4 1 4 4 4 4 2 3 1 4

 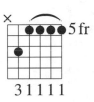 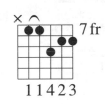 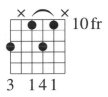 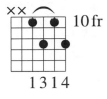

4 3 1 1 1 1 3 2 1 4 1 2 1 4 3 1 3 2 4 3 2 4 1 1 3 1 4

C6/E

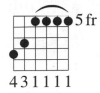 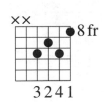  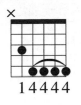 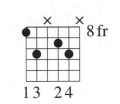

4231 2 3 1 4 3 1 1 1 1 2 3 1 4 1 1 4 2 3 3 1 4 1

C6/G

 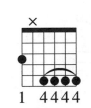 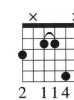 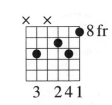 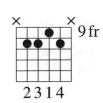 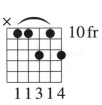

4 2 3 1 2 1 1 4 1 4 4 4 4 3 2 4 1 2 3 1 4 1 1 3 1 4

C6/A

  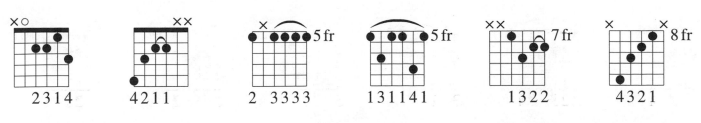

2 3 1 4 4 2 1 1 2 3 3 3 3 1 3 1 1 4 1 1 3 2 2 4 3 2 1

C5

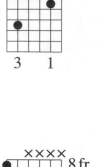

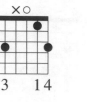
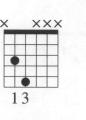
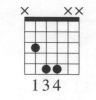
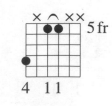
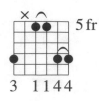

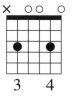
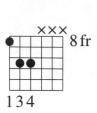
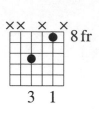
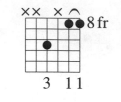
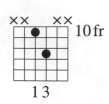
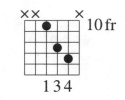

Csus2

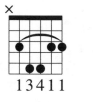
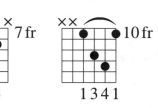
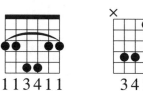

Csus2/G

Csus4

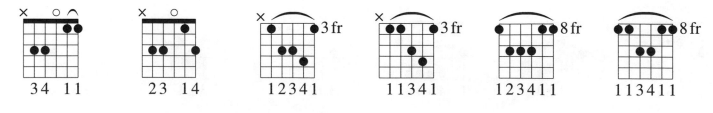

Csus4/G

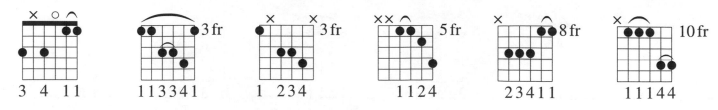

Cmaj7

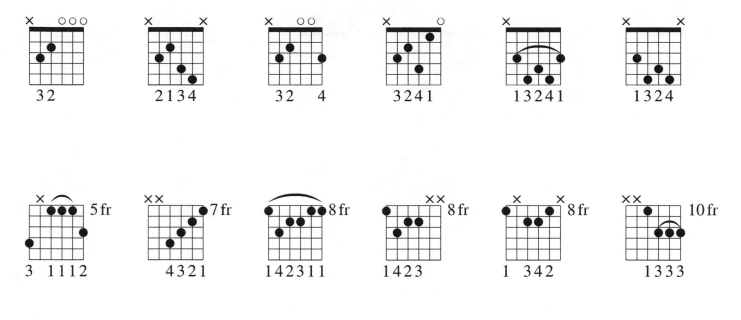

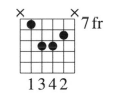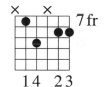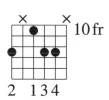

Cmaj7/E

Cmaj7/G

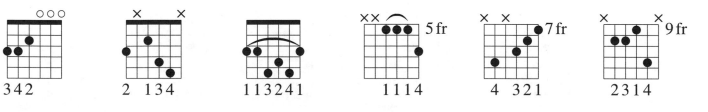

Cmaj7/B

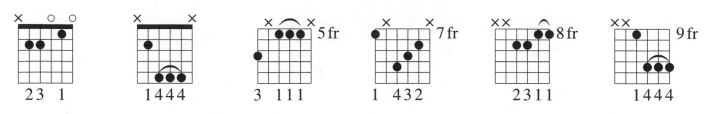

Cmaj7♭5

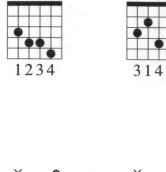

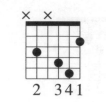
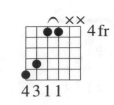
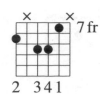

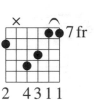
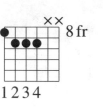
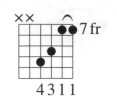
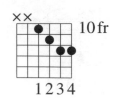
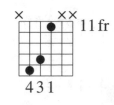

Cmaj7♭5/E

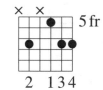
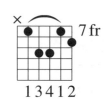
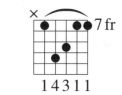
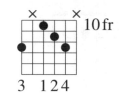
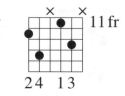

Cmaj7♭5/G♭

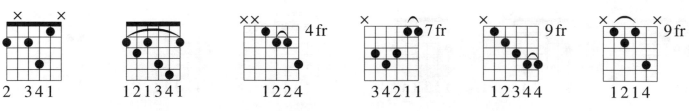

Cmaj7♭5/B

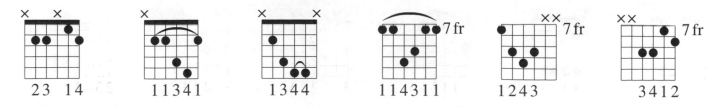

C(add9)

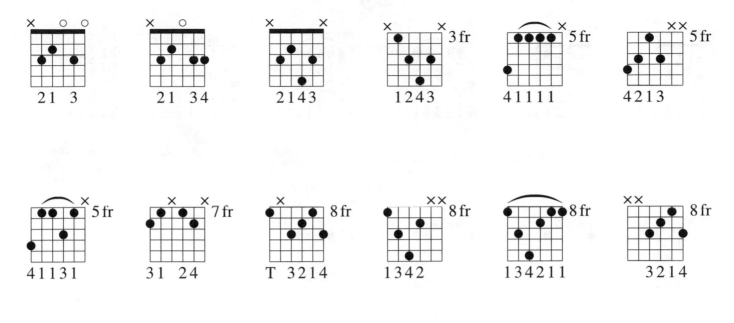

x o o
2 1 3

x o
2 1 3 4

x x
2 1 4 3

x ● ● x 3 fr
1 2 4 3

⌢ x 5 fr
4 1 1 1 1

x x 5 fr
4 2 1 3

⌢ x 5 fr
4 1 1 3 1

x x 7 fr
3 1 2 4

x x 8 fr
T 3 2 1 4

● x x 8 fr
1 3 4 2

⌢ x 8 fr
1 3 4 2 1 1

x x 8 fr
3 2 1 4

C(add9)/E

o o o
2 1 3

x x
1 4 2 3

x 5 fr
2 1 3 4 4

x ⌢ x 7 fr
1 4 1 2

⌢ 10 fr
2 1 1 3 4 1

⌢ 12 fr
1 4 1 1 2 1

C(add9)/G

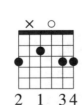

o x
2 3 1 4

x o
2 1 3 4

x x
2 1 4 3

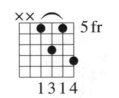

x x ⌢ 5 fr
1 3 1 4

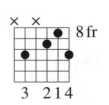

x x 8 fr
3 2 1 4

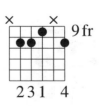

x x 9 fr
2 3 1 4

C(add9)/D

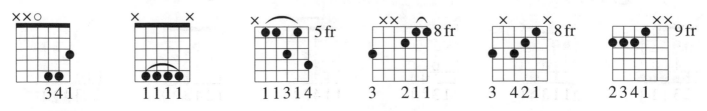

x x o
3 4 1

x x
1 1 1 1

x ⌢ 5 fr
1 1 3 1 4

x x ⌢ 8 fr
3 2 1 1

x x 8 fr
3 4 2 1

x x 9 fr
2 3 4 1

C$_9^6$

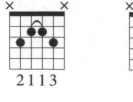
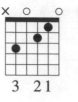

$\times$ · · $\times$ · · $\circ$ · $\circ$ · · · 5 fr · · · · · 5 fr · · $\times$ · · $\times$ · 5 fr · · · · 7 fr

2 1 1 3   3 2 1   4 1 2 3 1 1   4 1 1 1 1 1   4 2 3 1   2 1 1 1 4 4

2 1 3 4 4 7 fr   2 1 1 1 3 7 fr   2 1 1 1 3 4 7 fr   2 1 3 4 9 fr

C$_9^6$/E

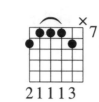
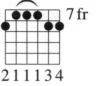

2 3 4   2 2 3 4 1 5 fr   1 1 1 2 7 fr   1 1 1 2 4 7 fr   3 1 4 1 1 10 fr   1 1 1 1 2 1 12 fr

C$_9^6$/G

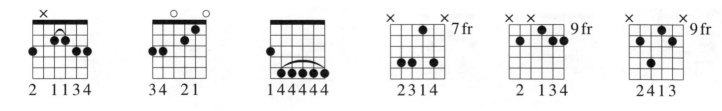

2 1 1 3 4   3 4 2 1   1 4 4 4 4 4   2 3 1 4 7 fr   2 1 3 4 9 fr   2 4 1 3 9 fr

C$_9^6$/D

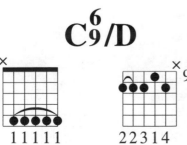

1 1 1 1 1   2 2 3 1 4 9 fr

C$_9^6$/A

1   1 4 2 2   1 3 2 4 7 fr

85

Cmaj9

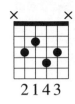
x   x
2 1 4 3

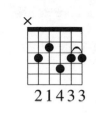
x
2 1 4 3 3

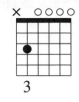
x   o o o o
3

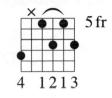
x   5 fr
4 1 2 1 3

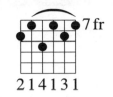
7 fr
2 1 4 1 3 1

7 fr
x
2 4 1 3 1

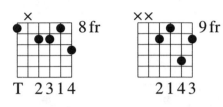
x
8 fr
T 2 3 1 4

9 fr
x x
2 1 4 3

Cmaj9/E

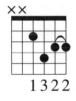
x x
1 3 2 2

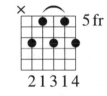
x   5 fr
2 1 3 1 4

7 fr
x   x
1 3 1 2

x   7 fr
1 4 1 2 1

x   10 fr
2 1 3 4 1

12 fr
x   x
1 3 1 1 2

Cmaj9/G

x   x
2 1 4 3

x   x
1 3   2 4

x x
2 4 1 3

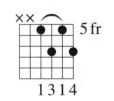
x x   5 fr
1 3 1 4

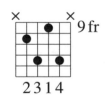
x   x   9 fr
2 3 1 4

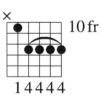
x   10 fr
1 4 4 4 4

Cmaj9/B

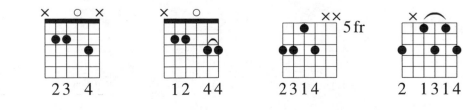
x   o o   o
2   4

x   o   x
2 3   4

x   o
1 2   4 4

x x 5 fr
2 3 1 4

x   5 fr
2 1 3 1 4

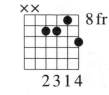
x x   8 fr
2 3 1 4

5-2 ALTERNATIVE MINOR CHORD FORMS

Cm

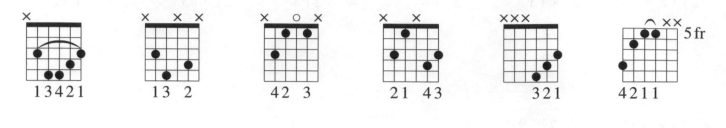

1 3 4 2 1   1 3   2   4 2   3   2 1   4 3   3 2 1   4 2 1 1

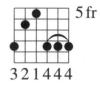 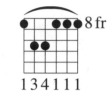 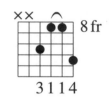 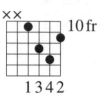 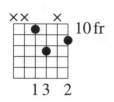

3 2 1 4 4 4   1 3 4 1 1 1   3 1 1 1   3 1 1 4   1 3 4 2   1 3   2

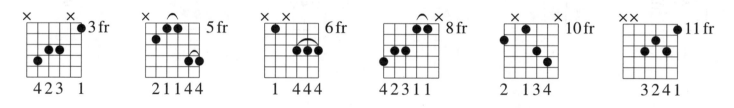

Cm/E♭

4 2 3   1   2 1 1 4 4   1   4 4 4   4 2 3 1 1   2   1 3 4   3 2 4 1

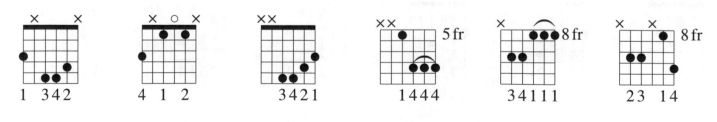

Cm/G

1   3 4 2   4   1   2   3 4 2 1   1 4 4 4   3 4 1 1 1   2 3   1 4

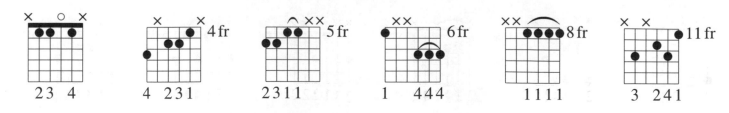

Cm/B♭

2 3   4   4   2 3 1   2 3 1 1   1   4 4 4   1 1 1 1   3   2 4 1

Cm6

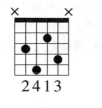 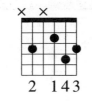 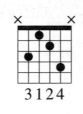 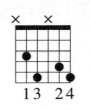 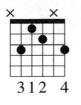

2 4 1 3	2 1 4 3	3 1 2 4	3 1 2 1 4	1 3 2 4	3 1 2 4

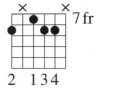 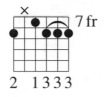 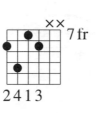 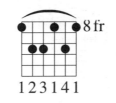 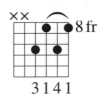 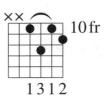

7 fr	7 fr	7 fr	8 fr	8 fr	10 fr
2 1 3 4	2 1 3 3 3	2 4 1 3	1 2 3 1 4 1	3 1 4 1	1 3 1 2

Cm6/E♭

 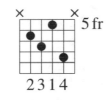 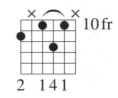 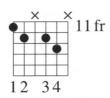

	5 fr	5 fr	6 fr	10 fr	11 fr
1 2 1 4	2 3 1 4	2 3 1 4 1	1 2 4 4 4	2 1 4 1	1 2 3 4

Cm6/G

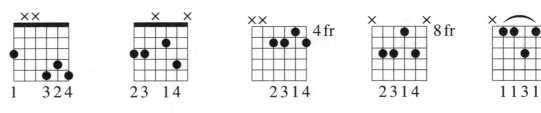

3 1 2 1	1 3 2 4	2 3 1 4	4 fr 2 3 1 4	8 fr 2 3 1 4	10 fr 1 1 3 1 2

Cm6/A

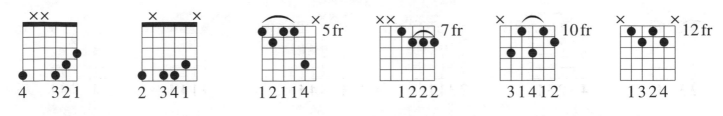

4 3 2 1	2 3 4 1	5 fr 1 2 1 1 4	7 fr 1 2 2 2	10 fr 3 1 4 1 2	12 fr 1 3 2 4

Cm7

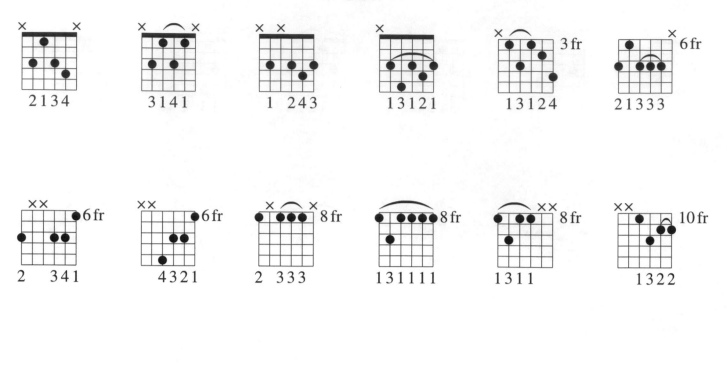

Cm7/E♭

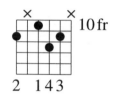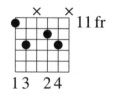

Cm7/G

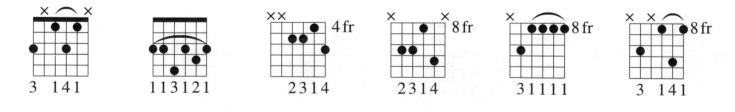

Cm7/B♭

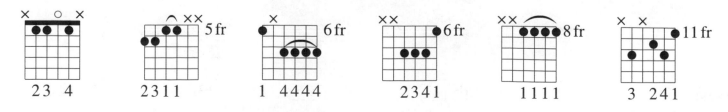

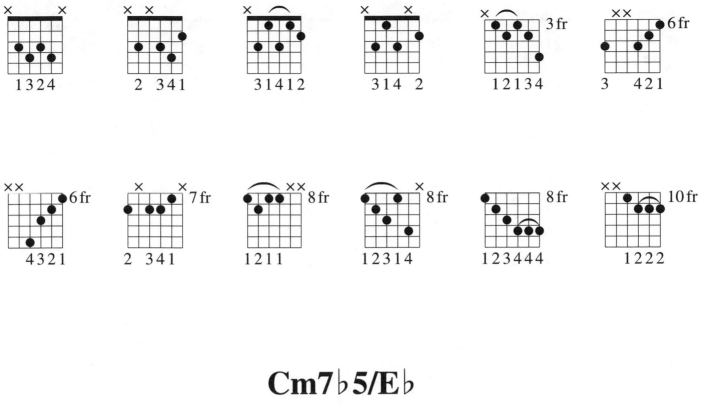

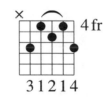
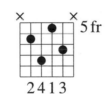
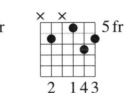
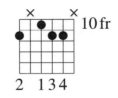
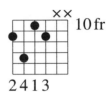

Cm7♭5/E♭

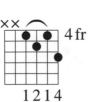
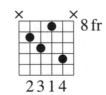
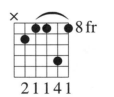

Cm7♭5/B♭

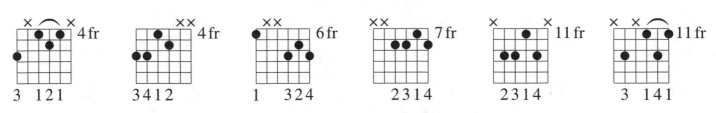

Cm(maj7)

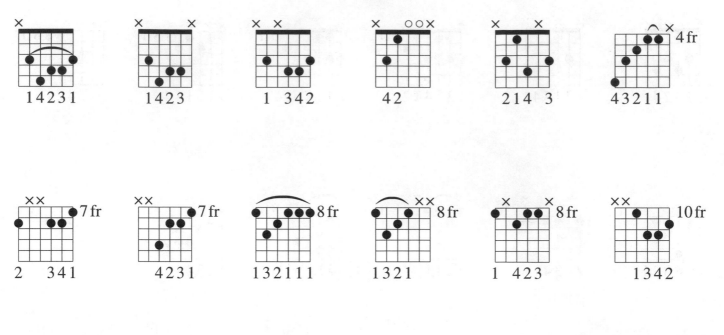

Cm(maj7)/E♭

Cm(maj7)/G

Cm(maj7)/B

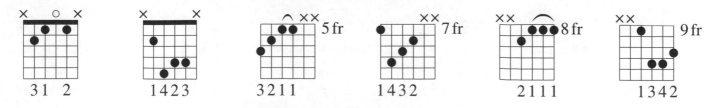

Cm(add9)

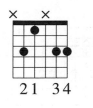 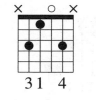 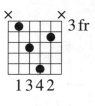 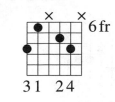 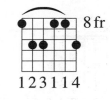 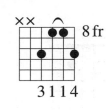

Cm(add9)/E♭

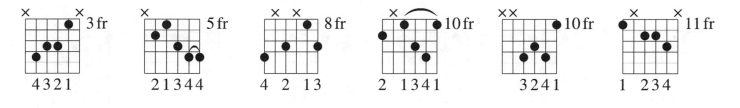

Cm(add9)/G

  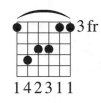 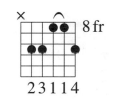 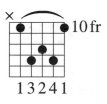

92

Cm$^6_9$

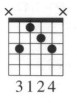
x   x

3 1 2 4

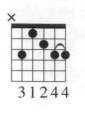
x

3 1 2 4 4

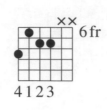
x x   6 fr

4 1 2 3

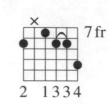
x   7 fr

2   1 3 3 4

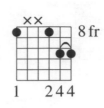
x x   8 fr

1   2 4 4

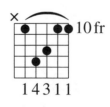
x x   8 fr

2 1 3 4

Cm$^6_9$/E♭

x x

1 2 4 4

x   5 fr

2 1 3 4 1

x   6 fr

1 2 3 4 4

x   10 fr

2   1 3 1 1

x x   10 fr

4 3 1 1

x   11 fr

1 2 2 2 4

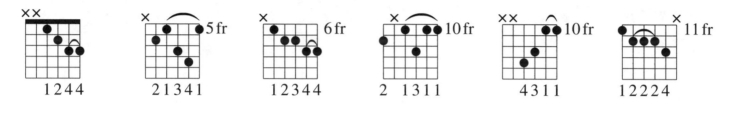

Cm$^6_9$/G

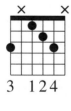
x   x

3   1 2 4

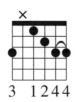
x

3   1 2 4 4

x x   4 fr

2 4 1 3

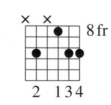
x   x   8 fr

2   1 3 4

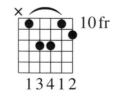
x   10 fr

1 3 4 1 2

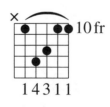
x   10 fr

1 4 3 1 1

92

Cm9

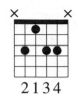 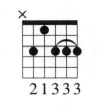 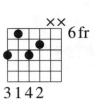 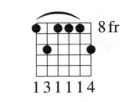

2 1 3 4   2 1 3 3 3   3 1 4 2   2 3 3 3 4   1 3 1 1 1 4   2 1 4 3

Cm9/E♭

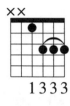 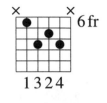 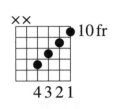 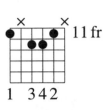

1 3 3 3   1 3 2 4   1 3 2 4   2 4 3 1   4 3 2 1   1 3 4 2

Cm9/G

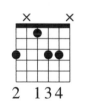 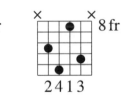 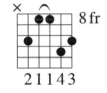 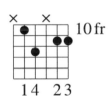

2 1 3 4   1 4 3 1 1 1   2 4 1 3   2 4 1 3   2 1 1 4 3   1 4 2 3

Cm9/B♭

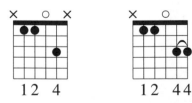 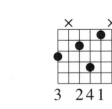 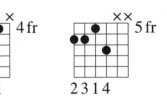 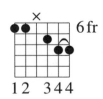 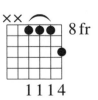

1 2 4   1 2 4 4   3 2 4 1   2 3 1 4   1 2 3 4 4   1 1 1 4

Cm9/D

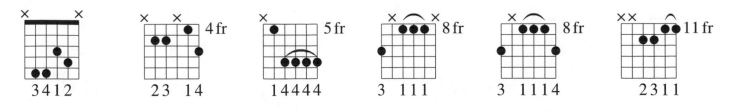

3 4 1 2   2 3 1 4   1 4 4 4 4   3 1 1 1   3 1 1 1 4   2 3 1 1

Cm11

 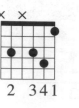 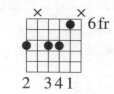 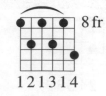 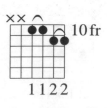

Cm11/E♭

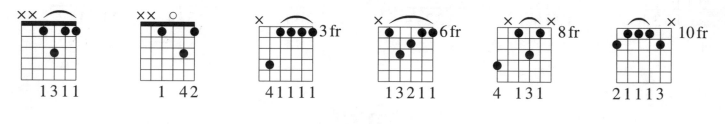

Cm11/G

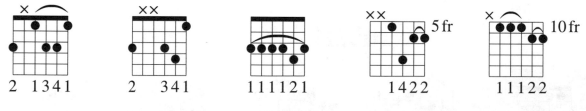 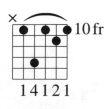

Cm11/B♭

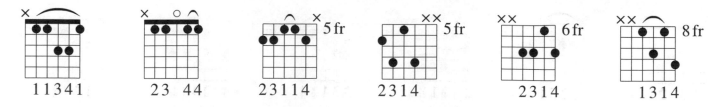

5-3 ALTERNATIVE DOM. 7 CHORD FORMS

C7

 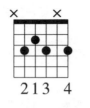 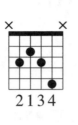 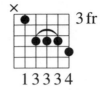

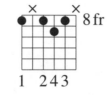 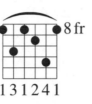 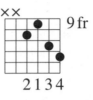 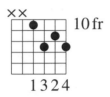

C7/E

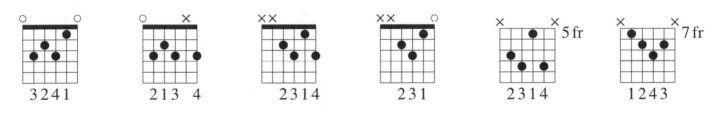

C7/G

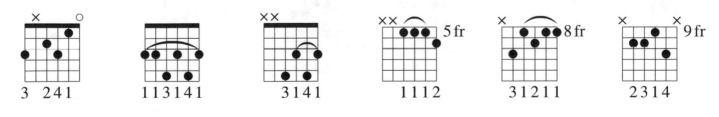

C7/B♭

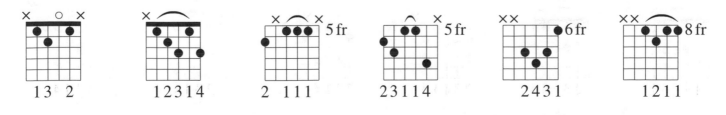

C7sus4

C7sus4/F

C7sus4/G

C7sus4/B♭

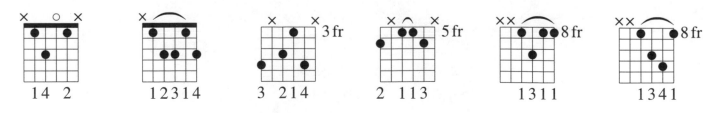

C7♭5

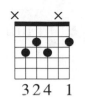 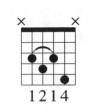 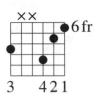 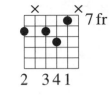  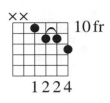

C7♭5/E

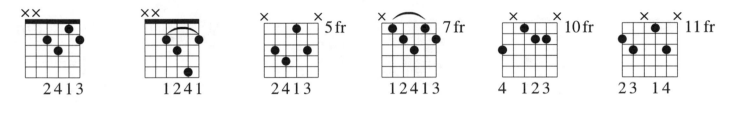

C7♭5/G♭

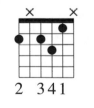 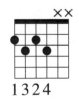 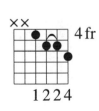 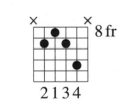 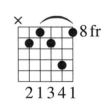 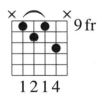

C7♭5/B♭

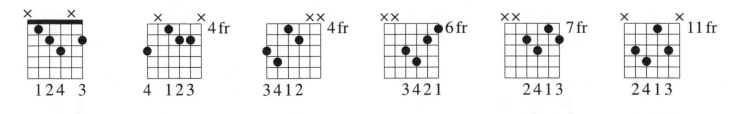

C7♯5

 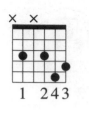 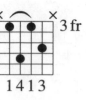 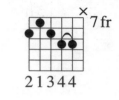 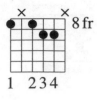 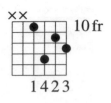

C7♯5/E

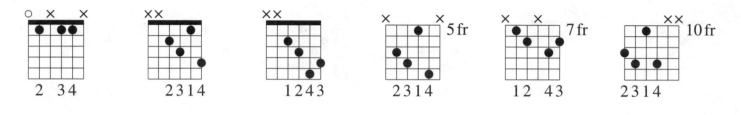

C7♯5/G♯

   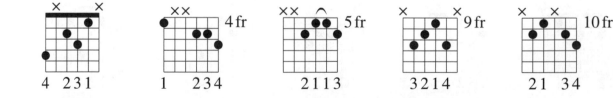 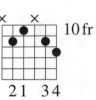

C7♯5/B♭

 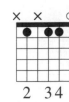 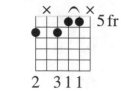 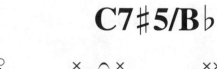 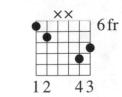 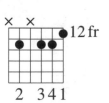

C9

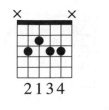 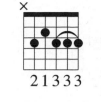 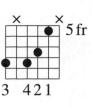 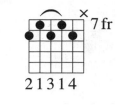 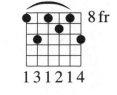 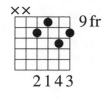

C9/E

C9/G

C9/B♭

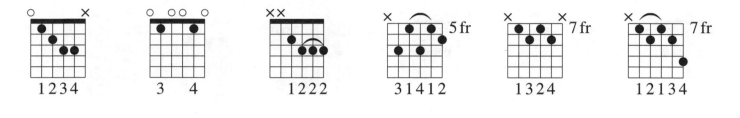

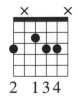 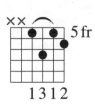 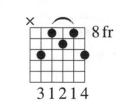 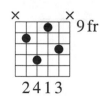 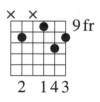

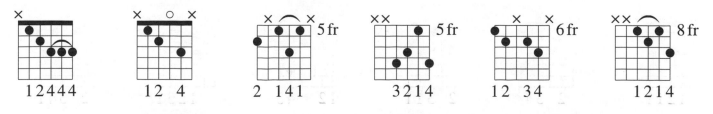

C9sus4

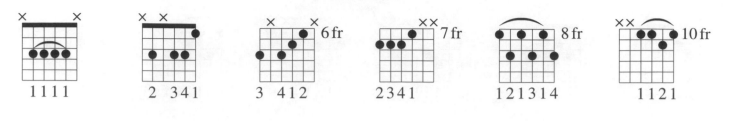

C9sus4/F

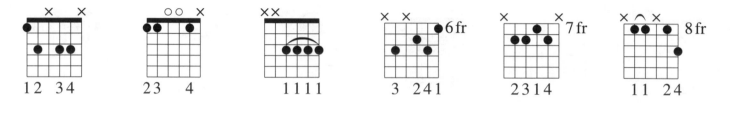

C9sus4/G

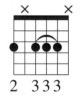 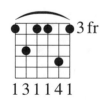 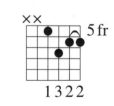 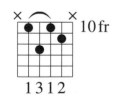 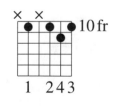

C9sus4/B♭

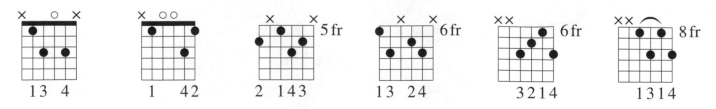

C7♭9

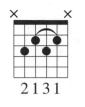
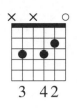
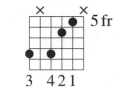
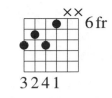
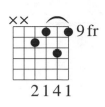

C7♭9/E

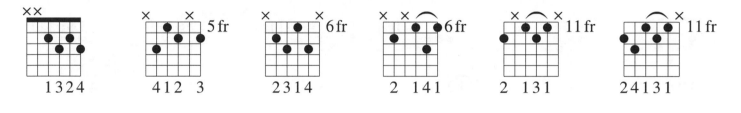

C7♭9/G

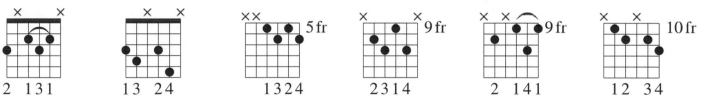

C7♭9/B♭

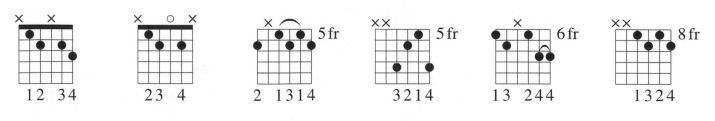

C7♯9

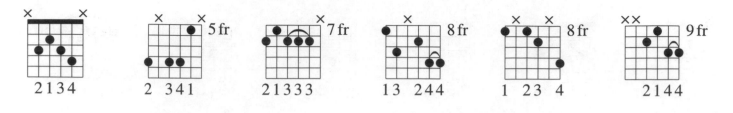

C7♯9/E

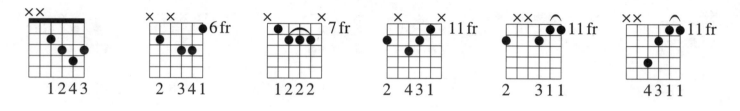

C7♯9/G

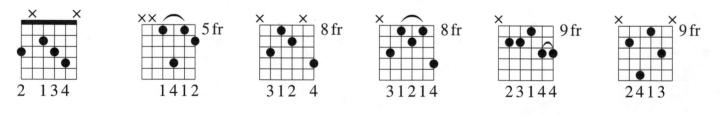

C7♯9/B♭

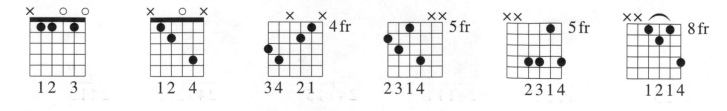

C11

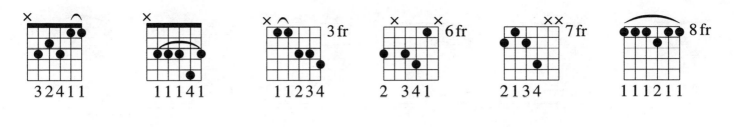

C11/E

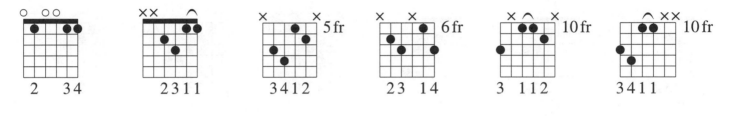

C11/F

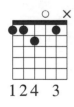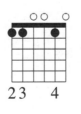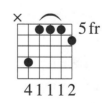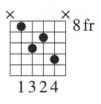

C11/B♭

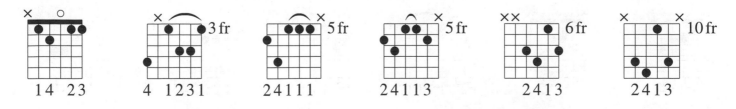

C13

2 1 3 3 4

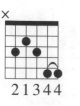
2 1 3 4 4

1 2 1 3 4

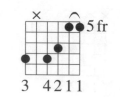
5 fr
3 4 2 1 1

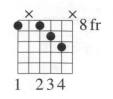
8 fr
1 2 3 4

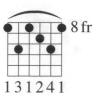
8 fr
1 3 1 2 4 1

C13/E

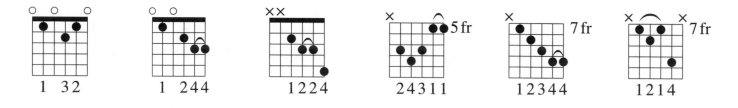

1 3 2

1 2 4 4

1 2 2 4

2 4 3 1 1
5 fr

1 2 3 4 4
7 fr

1 2 1 4
7 fr

C13/A

1 2 2 2

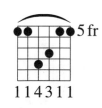
5 fr
1 1 4 3 1 1

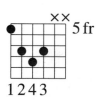
5 fr
1 2 4 3

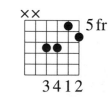
5 fr
3 4 1 2

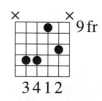
9 fr
3 4 1 2

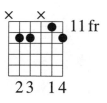
11 fr
2 3   1 4

C13/B♭

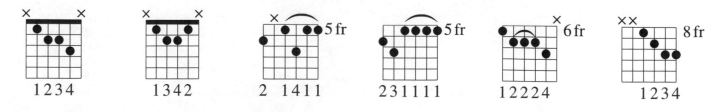

1 2 3 4

1 3 4 2

2 1 4 1 1
5 fr

2 3 1 1 1 1
5 fr

1 2 2 2 4
6 fr

1 2 3 4
8 fr

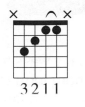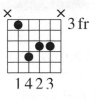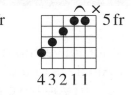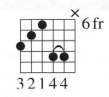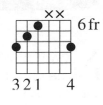

C+

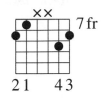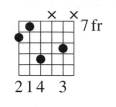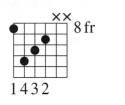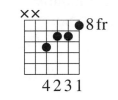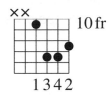

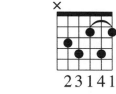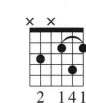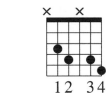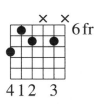

C°7

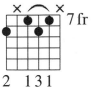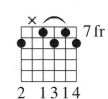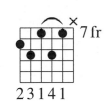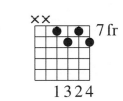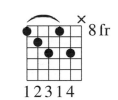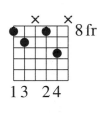

CHAPTER 5 REVIEW

Now that you've studied various alternative chord forms, you can imagine there are many ways to play the following exercises. Proximity is one of the key factors in selecting which chord form to use. Choose the one *nearest* to the chord you have just played so that the transition from one chord to another will be smooth. If the adjacent chords have common notes or similar fingerings, that would be even better. Do not overwhelm yourself, but experiment with as many combinations as possible and create a few that appeal to your ears the most. As before, write out an accompaniment for each progression and play it with a metronome.

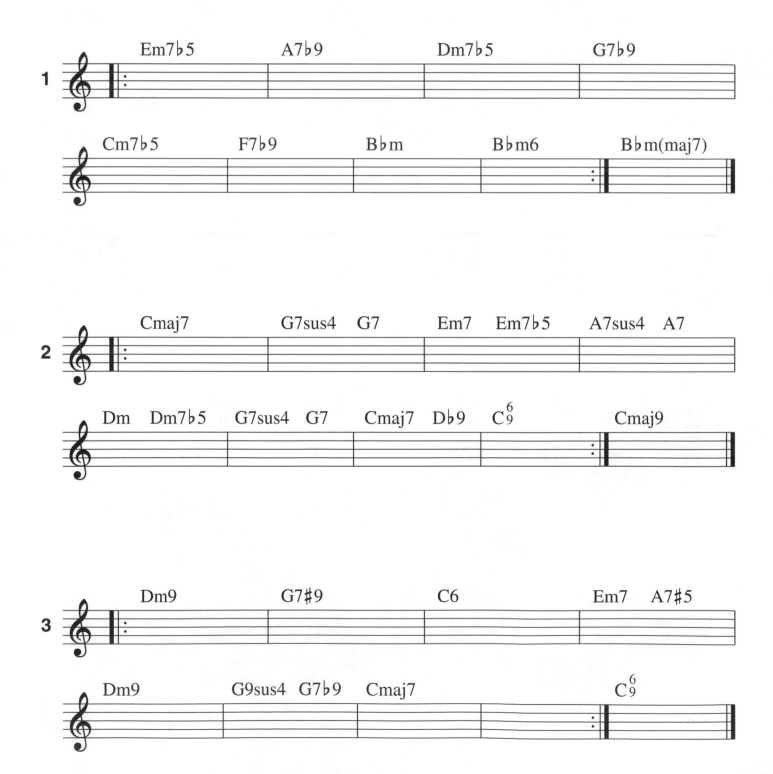

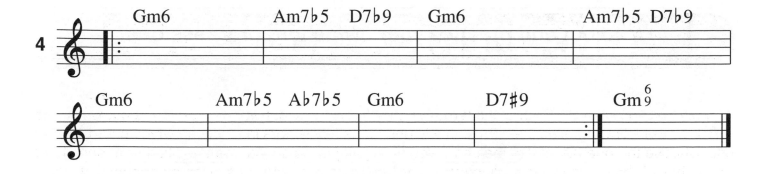

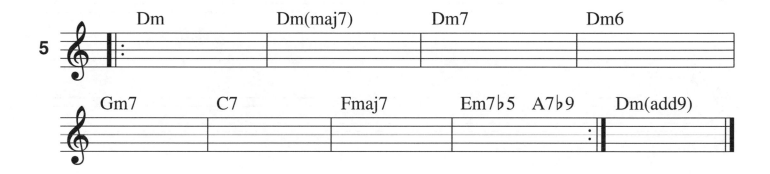

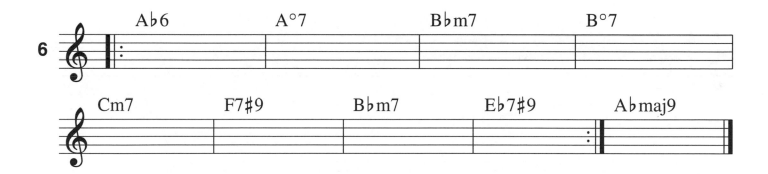

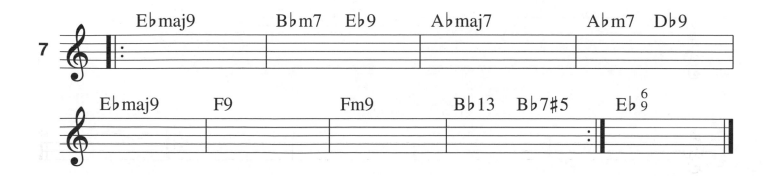

Write out and practice your own chord progressions.

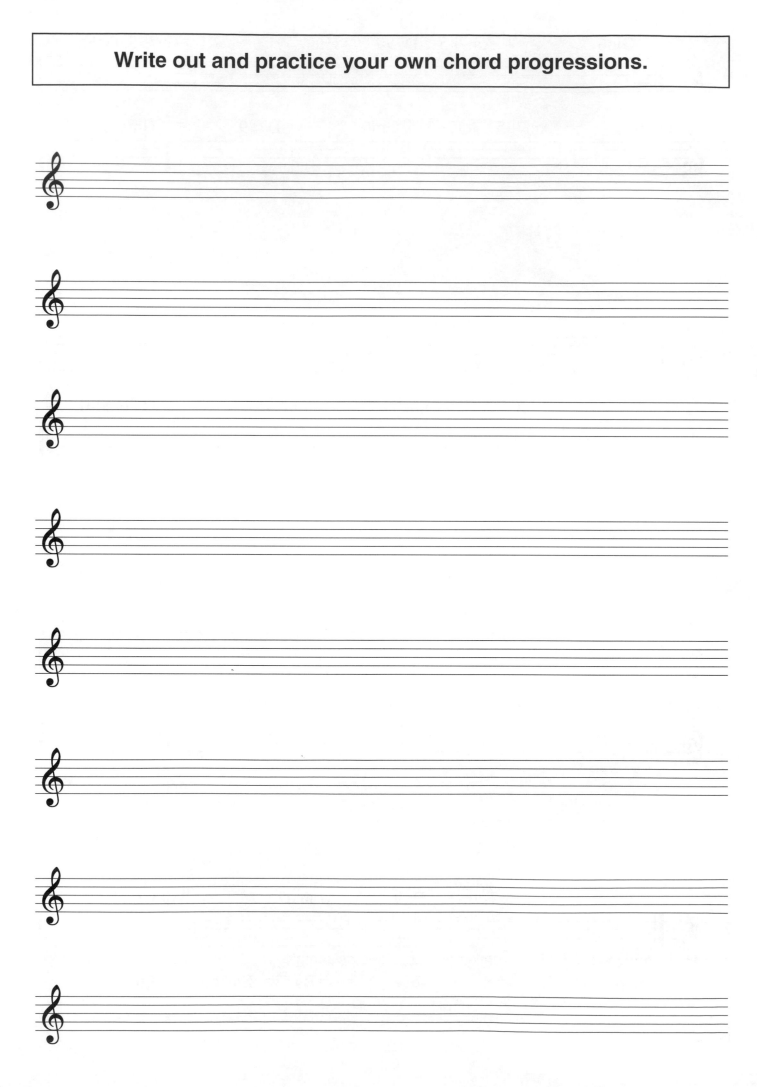

CHAPTER 6

ACCOMPANIMENT FOR VARIOUS MUSICAL STYLES

This chapter presents examples of accompaniment for selected musical styles, applying some of the chords and accompaniment patterns you have learned in both this book and *Guitar Chords and Accompaniment*. Each style is illustrated by one or more sample songs or short pieces of music with suggested chords and typical accompaniment examples. Also pay close attention to the music terms and elements you'll find, such as *styles, tempo, articulations,* and *dynamics*.

One of the main reasons you've learned a variety of guitar chords, accompaniment patterns, and basic theory is to be able to create and play some accompaniment when you have a simple lead sheet that only shows music, lyrics, and chord names. What chord forms or accompaniment styles to play, at what tempo a song should be played, and what dynamics are to be applied are some of the considerations you decide and plan before playing a song. This process of planning is called *arranging*. You've already done some arranging yourself whenever the book has instructed you in the exercises to write down your own accompaniment or try various chord forms. Some musicians write all the directions down, while others just decide what to do roughly in their head and then vary or improvise it during the performance. Each method has its own merit. And I suggest you practice both ways of arranging and play as many songs as possible while experimenting with various chord forms and accompaniment patterns. Although the topic of arranging can itself fill a book and is therefore beyond the scope of this book, here are some of the basic questions you should consider when arranging:

- What key should I play in? Should I transpose it to a key closer to my vocal range?

- What tempo should I play in—slow, medium, or fast?

- How should I mix various chord forms to make smooth chord transitions or add interest to the accompaniment?

- Should I strum throughout, or perhaps alternate between strumming and fingerpicking?

- How about adding some sections such as Intro, Interlude, Guitar Solo, or Ending?

- What dynamics—loud or soft—should I use in each section?

The songs and music that follow have been arranged as sample demonstrations of how the different styles of music can be played. Keep in mind, however, that each example is only one of many ways that you can play a song. By applying your own ideas, you can arrange and play them differently in your *own* original way—which is exactly what you have been encouraged to do throughout these two books!

6-1 BLUES STYLE

Blues developed from Afro-American spirituals and work songs that dealt with the hardships of everyday life and love. It is one of the oldest and most popular musical styles in the U.S. Two accompaniment styles typically played in blues are shown here in two popular keys, E and A. "Shuffle Me, Baby" presents an accompaniment in a *shuffled* rhythm based on eighth-note triplets, which you practiced in Section 3-8 of the introductory book. "Boogie Woogie Me, Baby" is in 12/8 and uses power chords throughout. The style is sometimes called *boogie-woogie*. You can slightly mute notes by lightly placing your right-hand palm on the strings, so they will not sound as loud or clear as when played without muting. Instead you will hear the notes *muffled*. The 12-bar song form shown here is the basis of most blues tunes and many songs in other musical styles such as rock, jazz, and country.

Shuffle Me, Baby

Boogie Woogie Me, Baby

Moderately slow

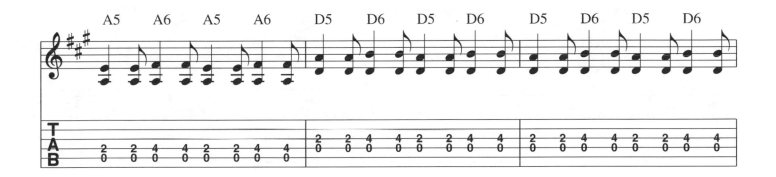

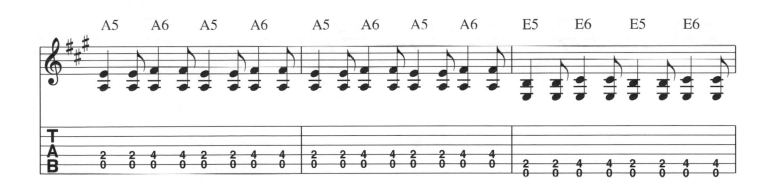

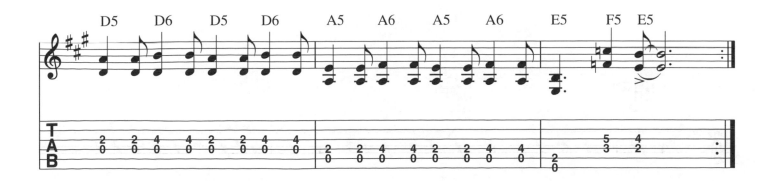

6-2 ROCK STYLE

Here are three accompaniment examples in various styles of rock. "Billy" presents the early rock-and-roll style of the '50s and early '60s sometimes called *rockabilly,* which was based on rhythm-and-blues and country. It was popularized by such musicians as Elvis Presley, Chuck Berry, Scotty Moore, and Carl Perkins. "Hear Me Out" is arranged in a slightly more contemporary rock style based mostly on the sixteenth-note rhythms that became more common after the '70s. The accompaniment to "Aura Lee" exemplifies the typical early-rock ballad style, which is to be played at a slow tempo. For all three tunes, experiment with different chord forms and accompaniment patterns.

Billy

Hear Me Out

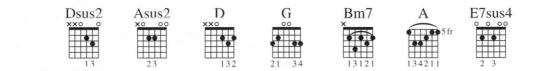

Medium Rock ♩ = 92

Repeat 3 times

Aura Lee

Slowly, with expression

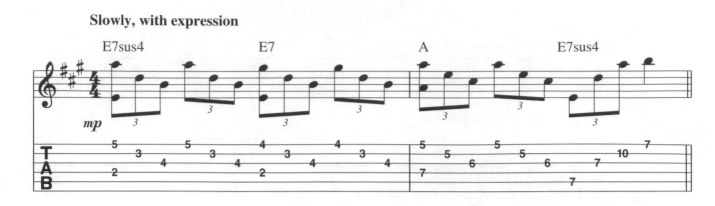

1. As the black-bird in the spring be-neath the wil-low
2., 3., 4. See Additional Lyrics

tree   Sat and piped I heard him sing, and

sing of Au-ra Lee.   Au - ra Lee,

Additional Lyrics

2. On her cheek the rose was born, 'twas music when she spake.
   In her eyes the rays of morn with sudden splendor break.
   Aura Lee, Aura Lee, maid of golden hair.
   Sunshine came along with thee, and swallows in the air.

3. Aura Lee, the bird may flee the willow's golden hair,
   Swing through winter fitfully on cold and stormy air.
   Yet if thine eyes I see, gloom will soon depart.
   For to me sweet Aura Lee is sunshine through my heart.

4. When the mistletoe was green amidst the winter's snows,
   Sunshine in thy face was seen and kissing lips of rose.
   Aura Lee, Aura Lee, take my golden ring.
   Love and light return with thee, and swallows with the spring.

6-3 FOLK STYLE

Here's a familiar tune, "Long, Long Ago," arranged in folk or folk-rock style. Notice it is written in cut time and the accompaniment is based on several fingerpicking patterns.

Long, Long Ago

Now you are come, all my grief is re - moved.

Let me for - get that so long you have roved.

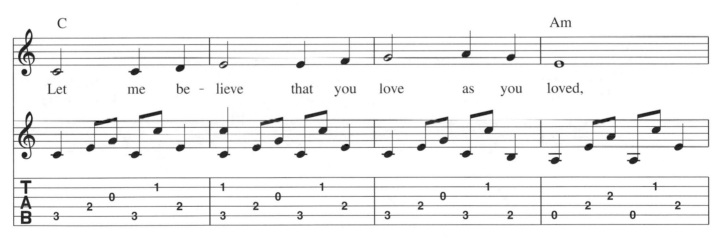

Let me be - lieve that you love as you loved,

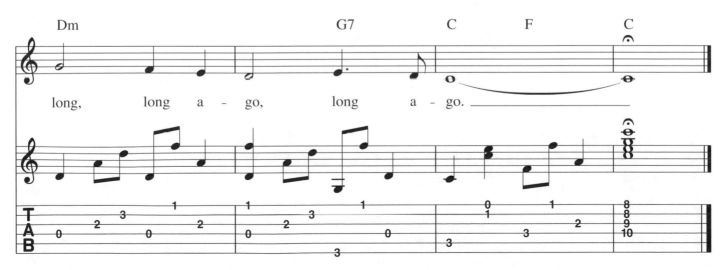

long, long a - go, long a - go.

6-4 COUNTRY STYLE

Below is "She'll Be Comin' 'Round the Mountain" arranged in an accompaniment style typically played in country music. It incorporates the *Carter Family* style throughout and is played at a fairly bright tempo in cut time. Slow down or play one bass note for each chord if you have difficulty alternating between the bass notes and strumming.

She'll Be Comin' 'Round the Mountain

Cheerfully ♩ = 120

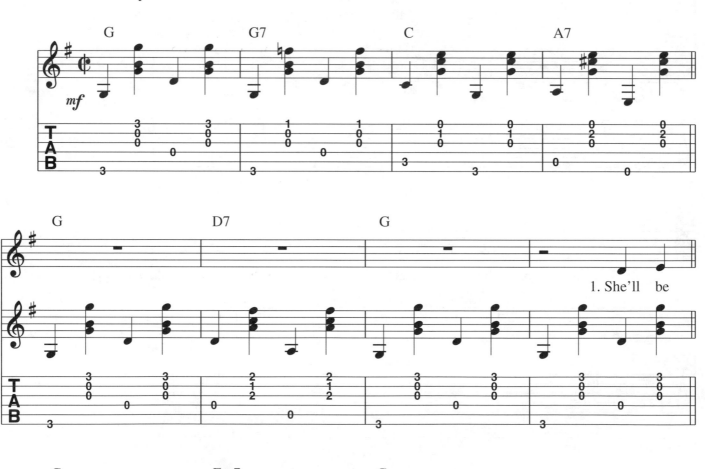

Additional Lyrics

2. She'll be drivin' six white horses when she comes.
   She'll be drivin' six white horses when she comes.
   She'll be drivin' six white horses, she'll be drivin' six white
   Horses, she'll be drivin' six white horses when she comes.

3. Oh, we'll all go out to meet her when she comes.
   Oh, we'll all go out to meet her when she comes.
   Oh, we'll all go out to meet her, oh, we'll all go out to meet
   Her, oh, we'll all go out to meet her when she comes.

4. She'll be shinin' just like silver when she comes.
   She'll be shinin' just like silver when she comes.
   She'll be shinin' just like silver, she'll be shinin' just like
   Silver, she'll be shinin' just like silver when she comes.

5. She'll be breathin' smoke and fire when she comes.
   She'll be breathin' smoke and fire when she comes.
   She'll be breathin' smoke and fire, she'll be breathin' smoke
   And fire, she'll be breathin' smoke and fire when she comes.

6-5 CLASSICAL STYLE

Here is a song arranged for solo classical guitar style in 3/8. In a strict sense, it is not an accompaniment since there is no vocal or other instruments to accompany. However, it should present a good exercise for practicing arpeggios and playing in 3/8 meter. As traditionally done in classical guitar music, there are no chord symbols or frames. However, TAB is given here as a reference. Go through each measure slowly. Create fingerings that allow for smooth and easy chord transitions. As you will notice, each arpeggio is based on a chord you already know. Once you identify the chord, hold it as long as you can and strive for legato playing throughout. If you have difficulty synchronizing the upper and lower parts, practice each part separately at first. Then combine and play the two parts together very slowly when you are ready.

Three-Eighth Waltz

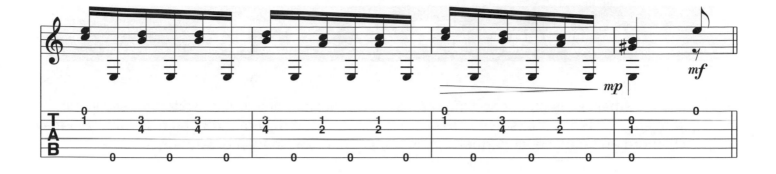

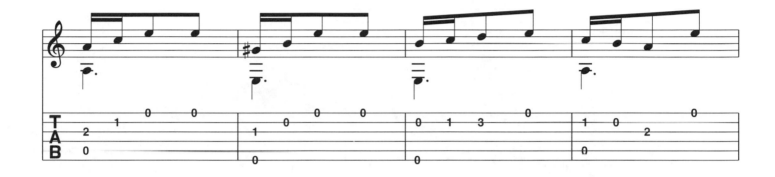

6-6 JAZZ STYLE

Here is a 12-bar blues composed in jazz idiom. The accompaniment is written mostly in simple quarter-note slashes, but strive to keep a steady time and rhythm throughout. In jazz, you may find each chord and the overall harmony slightly more complex than in other musical styles.

Instant Blues

6-7 LATIN STYLE

The accompaniment styles shown in this section exemplify some of the popular Latin musical styles: *reggae*, *beguine*, *rhumba*, and *mambo*. You will see some basic patterns typical of each style, followed by a short sample of music.

REGGAE

Reggae is a musical style based on a Jamaican rhythm combined with early rhythm-and-blues and a bit of calypso. Though popular on its own, it's also sometimes incorporated into other styles of music such as rock, jazz, and fusion.

Basic Patterns

Example

BEGUINE

Having originated in the French West Indies, *beguine* has strongly Spanish-influenced rhythms. The example uses the third basic pattern. Watch out for accents and alternating bass.

Basic Patterns

Example

RHUMBA (or RUMBA)

Rhumba or *rumba* was first introduced in the U.S. from Cuba in the 1930s. Use barre chords instead of open chords to execute *mute* (written by X) more easily.

Basic Patterns

Example

MAMBO

Mambo is another popular and lively Cuban musical style usually played with big horns. Watch out for those ties and try not to rush when playing the basic patterns.

Basic Patterns

Example

WHAT'S NEXT?

If you have been diligently studying and practicing *Guitar Chords and Accompaniment* and this book, you have gained a good, extensive vocabulary of guitar chords and various accompaniment patterns and styles. Here are some suggestions regarding what you can do next:

1. Choose your favorite chords and organize them in your own chord note-book. Do not limit yourself only to those presented here. You will be pleased to know that although these two books have covered a wide variety of guitar chords, there are more chords and alternative chord forms you can further explore.

2. Start creating your *own* accompaniment patterns based on those you have learned. As you practice, you can modify or combine several patterns in any way you like and create something new from scratch.

3. Go back to each song provided in both this book and *Guitar Chords and Accompaniment* and rearrange it in any way you like. You can, for example, change the key, accompaniment patterns, tempo, or chord forms. Or you can add such new sections as an Intro or Interlude. Select as many songs as you want from a songbook and practice arranging and playing every day.

4. Select and study your favorite style of music for a period of time. For instance, if you like rock, listen to as many rock guitar players as you can and start emulating what they play on CDs. If you are interested in learning jazz, go to jazz clubs or listen on the radio and pay attention to how various musicians accompany one another. You can also check out *Jazz Guitar Chords and Accompaniment* (ISBN: 1-891370-07-3).

5. When you can play a song or two and feel ready, go out and play for someone. You can form a band or play solo, but start playing for your mom, dad, friends or anybody! It's not only a lot of fun, but you'll also get valuable feedback—positive and negative—that will motivate you in many useful ways.

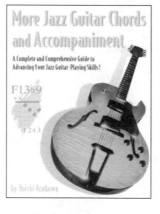

QUESTIONNAIRE

Thank you for your purchase of *More Guitar Chords and Accompaniment* (2nd ed.). Your suggestions, questions, and comments are greatly appreciated. Please take the time to fill out this questionnaire and send it to: **SIX STRINGS MUSIC PUBLISHING, P.O. Box 7718, Torrance, CA 90504-9118.**

1. Where did you purchase this book?

2. How long have you been playing the guitar?

3. If you are a teacher, how long have you been teaching? What other books have you used?

4. Which music magazines do you read regularly?

5. What music books (instructional or personal folios) do you use and like?

6. What kinds of music books would you like to see in the future?

7. What is your favorite type of music? Who is your favorite musician or music group?

8. Comments or suggestions regarding this book:

NAME: _____ **AGE:** _____

ADDRESS: _____

CITY: _____ **STATE:** _____ **ZIP:** _____

ORDER FORM

ISBN #	Titles	Qty	Price	Subtotal
			$	$
			$	$
			$	$
			$	$

Subtotal	$
Residents of Los Angeles County—8.25% sales tax Other residents of California—7.25% sales tax	$
Shipping & handling ($5.50 for the first book, plus $1.25 for each additional book)	$
TOTAL	$

PAYMENT

❑ **CHECK** or **MONEY ORDER** (U.S. ONLY)

Please send this order form with your check or money order to:
SIX STRINGS MUSIC PUBLISHING, P.O. Box 7718, Torrance, CA 90504-9118

❑ **CREDIT CARD:** ○ **Visa**   ○ **MasterCard**   ○ **American Express**

Mail this order form, *or* fax it to **310-324-8544,** *or* call toll-free **800-784-0203**.

Card number: _____

Name on card: _____ Exp. date: _____

❑ **INTERNET:** You can also order on-line at **http://www.sixstringsmusicpub.com**

Note: Prices subject to change without notice. No C.O.D. orders, please.

MAILING ADDRESS

NAME: _____ AGE: _____

ADDRESS: _____

CITY: _____ STATE: _____ ZIP: _____

TEL: _____ E-MAIL: _____